THE HIPPEST TRIP IN AMERICA

ALSO BY NELSON GEORGE

FICTION

Urban Romance

Seduced

One Woman Short

Show & Tell

Night Work

The Accidental Hunter

The Plot Against Hip Hop

Nonfiction

Where Did Our Love Go: The Rise and Fall of the Motown Sound

The Death of Rhythm & Blues

Elevating the Game

Blackface

Buppies, B-Boys, Baps & Bohos: Notes on Post-Soul Black Culture

The James Brown Reader: 50 Years of Writing About the Godfather of Soul (edited with Alan Leeds)

City Kid: A Memoir

THE HIPPEST TRIP
IN AMERICA

SOUL
TRAIN AND THE EVOLUTION
OF CULTURE AND STYLE

NELSON GEORGE

WILLIAM MORROW
An Imprint of HarperCollins*Publishers*

HarperCollins books may be purchased for educational, business, or sales promotional use. For information please e-mail the Special Markets Department at SPsales@harpercollins.com.

FIRST EDITION

Chapter opener image © by Ron Dale/Shutterstock, Inc.

Designed by Lisa Stokes

Library of Congress Cataloging-in-Publication Data has been applied for.

ISBN 978-0-06-222103-2

14 15 16 17 18 OV/RRD 10 9 8 7 6 5 4 3 2 1

To all who have danced on a Soul Train *line anywhere in the world*

CONTENTS

||||||||||||||||||||||||||||||||||

INTRODUCTION

|||||||||||||||||||||||||||||||||

ON FEBRUARY 3, 2012, I got off the subway at Forty-second Street in bustling midtown Manhattan and rolled up toward Duffy Square, a section defined by garish red elevated seats and a glitzy booth where cut-rate tickets for Broadway shows are sold. The New York City police had set up barricades along a section of Broadway, which in the last decade had been converted into a Times Square pedestrian mall. Today this whole area was filled with women and men wearing Afro wigs, long coats, silver platform shoes, round granny glasses, and other flashbacks to fly 1970s gear. The crowd—about a thousand or so folks—was made up of wannabe dancers and cell phone–carrying onlookers. The weather was unusually mild, and that put the attend-ees in a festive mood, even though we were at a wake for a beloved cultural figure and his iconic television show.

Don Cornelius had died two days earlier. His legacy was strong and undeniable. He had created a television show that ran from Octo-ber 2, 1971, to March 26, 2006—thirty-five years of "love, peace, and *soul*" resulting in countless contributions to our collective popular culture. The show was called *Soul Train*, and Cornelius's death brought about even bigger flash mobs in *Soul Train*'s hometown of Chicago and in Philadelphia, where a *Soul Train* line was organized that would make the *Guinness Book of World Records*.

But what the New York gathering lacked in numbers it made up for in enthusiasm. An old-school dancer organized the chaos into a line that ran about a hundred feet. It wasn't as flashy or dynamic as the *Soul Train* lines you can revisit on YouTube. Nothing done today can recapture that vitality. But the dozens who boogied down the line, and in ad hoc groups around Duffy Square, did so with love and a whole lot of joy.

I didn't dance down the line. Modesty and good sense kept me on the sidelines. But the whole scene did flash me back to many childhood Saturday mornings when my sister and I would sit in front of our family's small color TV and, like thousands of other folks, watch our favorite soul singers and funk bands perform while an amazing crew of dancers gyrated and percolated to the latest hits. The *Soul Train* line, always near the end of the show, was a highlight. Every show, the dancers would bust out new moves that would be imitated at parties across the country later that night.

On that day in February, we had all gathered to celebrate the life of Don Cornelius, that man with the deep voice and the remarkable wardrobe, who had taken his own life with a shotgun in his Los Angeles home. Though shocked by his suicide, the folks in the New York *Soul Train* line, as in the lines in Chicago and Philadelphia, weren't sober. They had more in common with the exuberant second-line celebrations of New Orleans than anything mournful. Don Cornelius had brought us joy, and it was with joy he was remembered.

Saturday mornings in the 1970s, back in the kitchen of my family's Brooklyn housing project, I'd sit alongside my little sister, eat a bowl of Cap'n Crunch cereal, and watch *Soul Train*—complete with scintillating dancers, soul music's finest performers, and an ultracool host—on our rabbit-ear TV. It was a music show that not only generated hit records but also connected all of black (and a hip section of white, Latino, and Asian) America into a groovy community.

In the pages ahead, you'll hear a lot of anecdotes like mine—tales of Saturday-morning rituals built around the show that, like the insistent rhythm of a great song, will connect you to the joy that was *Soul Train*'s unique combination of music, dance, and personality. These ingredients made *Soul Train* both one of the longest-running shows in television history and an iconic cultural touchstone for folks not born during its heyday. Somehow *Soul Train* has soaked into the DNA of our pop culture. The details of its creation, the rituals it embodied for viewers and participants, and the social and media context in which it existed are all part of the story I'll tell.

For casual readers as well as longtime fans, I view this book as a platform for further exploration. I'll mention specific shows and performances with an eye toward inspiring readers to follow up on what intrigues them via YouTube or *Soul Train* fan sites. The foundation of this book comes from the interviews conducted for VH1's 2010 documentary *The Hippest Trip in America*, which captured the flavor of the show but, because of time constraints, only used small portions of the interview material.

I interviewed Don Cornelius many times in the 1980s. On my first trip to Los Angeles I flew out from New York to attend the Black Music Association convention. The organization was a well-intentioned attempt to pull together the culture's various branches—record labels, radio stations, retail, concert promotion, performers—into a coherent business and social force. While the convention hardly fulfilled its lofty goal and the group has long been defunct, I did get a chance to visit the set of *Soul Train*. I have vivid memories of DeBarge, the family vocal group from Grand Rapids, Michigan, exiting a van and heading onto a soundstage for a taping.

Any glamour I'd associated with the tapings was quickly dissipated by the sight of the dancers, most my age or younger (I was twenty-four), looking tired as they impatiently waited for the next act to appear.

When I finally met Don he was cordial, though he didn't go out of his way to make me feel comfortable. I could feel him sizing me up. Was I a possible ally, or a too-smart-for-my-own-good asshole? The lack of outward warmth (a quality often manufactured by Hollywood hustlers on first encounters) stuck out, but so did Don's forthright answers to my questions and his consummate confidence. My memory of that encounter with Don is very similar to the memories of others that you'll read throughout the book. Don's bearing, voice, and manner were consistent throughout the years, as we'll learn from scores of people who spent time with him—from dancers, musicians, and staff to business partners and friends, from the 1960s until his death. Don's controlled demeanor and unrelenting cool made him hard to know and difficult to get close to, but those who knew him well testify to a funnier, looser man than he revealed to the public.

Don was defined more by his actions than he was by anything he said about himself. Inspired by the civil rights movement, he saw a space for black joy on television. He believed that the music and dance of "negroes" would be as captivating on the tube as it was in a Chicago house party. He was definitely a "race man," but he built professional alliances across racial lines with syndicators, advertisers, and record labels. In the process, he empowered many other black businesspeople while introducing the post–civil rights generation of white consumers to the dynamic power of black music.

As much as *Soul Train* was Don's show, it was also owned spiritually by the dancers whose creativity and excitement leaped off the TV screen each week. How they got on the show, the moves they made, and the show's effect on their lives are very much the backbone of this story. So many dynamic dancers passed in front of the show's cameras that it would be impossible to capture them all. Only a few are explored in depth here.

So let's go back in time to the tumultuous years of the civil rights movement and the Windy City streets where the hawk—known also as the Chicago wind—blew hard and long. Pull up the collar on your maxi coat, slide into your platform shoes, and pump that Afro Sheen into your hair.

As Don so often said, "You can bet your last money . . . it's gonna be a stone gas, honey!"

THE HIPPEST TRIP IN AMERICA

Chapter 1
WINDY CITY

||||||||||||||||||||||||||||||||||

One of the problems during the period when we started Soul Train *was the lack of opportunity for black talent on television. I'm talking the sixties and part of the seventies. It was a medium that didn't feature minorities as much as it could have. And it was a medium that didn't feature minorities in a positive way as opposed to a negative way . . . it bothered me personally and that's kind of why I wanted to get a spot on television. So that maybe I could do something about presenting black people in particular in a positive way.*

—DON CORNELIUS, 2009

THE LANDSCAPE of black images on television and in film in the mid-1960s was pretty barren. I'm not sure anyone who came of age in the 1980s or beyond will ever understand how absent "negro" faces were once on television in America. There was no Winfrey network. No Steve Harvey talk show. No argumentative sportscasters like Stephen A. Smith. The news broadcasts were when a dark face could be seen protesting, or an angry Malcolm X or an inspiring Dr. King or a local civil rights activist being interviewed about "the negro problem."

But as far as entertainment went, Sammy Davis Jr. was one of the few blacks who was a regular on network variety shows, largely because he was part of Frank Sinatra's revered Rat Pack. An act from

Berry Gordy's Motown Records stable, like the Supremes, the Temptations, or the Four Tops, popped up on *American Bandstand, Shindig,* or other teen-appeal music shows singing "the sound of young America" and executing exquisite choreography. Crossover comic Bill Cosby costarred on the NBC series *I Spy* for several years in the mid-1960s, the foundation of his long successful TV career.

In September 1968 the lovely Diahann Carroll was made the lead in *Julia,* a half-hour NBC sitcom in which she portrayed a single mother and nurse. While its existence was groundbreaking, the show's writing and plotting was bland. Moreover, during all of the show's eighty-six episodes, the team behind *Julia* was as lily-white as the rest of America's big three networks.

At the time *Julia* was cautiously opening the network TV door, Donald Cortez Cornelius was already on his journey toward pop-culture immortality. Unlike a lot of prominent black figures who emerged in the civil rights years, Cornelius wasn't a southern immigrant to the north, but a native son of one of America's biggest cities. He was born on September 27, 1936, in Chicago's Bronzeville, a densely packed, segregation-created black community on the city's South Side. Two of the greatest works of postwar black literature were set on these same tough streets: Richard Wright's *Native Son* (1940), which features a restless young man named Bigger Thomas whose life ended tragically, and Lorraine Hansberry's *A Raisin in the Sun* (1959), which featured a restless young man named Walter Lee Younger who made mistakes in search of a better life for his family. Wright's bestseller was draped in despair, while Hansberry saw a brighter future in the face of racism. Perhaps the difference between the two characters is the difference between America in 1940 and 1959.

Don was twenty-three years old in 1959 when Hansberry's play first appeared. He must have shared its optimism and, thankfully, was way more Walter Lee than Bigger. He attended one of the city's most important black high schools, DuSable (named after the black trader who founded Chicago), and after graduation he joined the Marine Corps and served in Korea for eighteen months. He married Delores Harrison in 1956 and quickly had two sons, Anthony and Raymond. His personal ambition can be seen in the jobs he worked prior to moving into media: he sold tires and automobiles, briefly was a policeman, and dabbled in insurance—a rapid journey from blue to white collar in the space of a few years.

He was tall and handsome, and it wasn't long before that foghorn voice gave him the idea of doing radio. In 1966 he took a three-month radio course, and a year later he landed a job at Chicago's WVON, one of the greatest of the rhythm and blues radio stations that were the backbone of black music and the communities they served.

These are the early biographical details of Don Cornelius, but we can't introduce him without also discussing the quasi-mystical, mid-century quality popularly known as "cool." Professor Robert Farris Thompson, a historian of West African culture, traces the concept of "cool" to Yoruba and Igbo civilizations. Thompson has argued that "The telling point is that the 'mask' of coolness is worn not only in times of stress, but also but in times of pleasure . . . I have come to term the attitude 'an aesthetic of the cool' in the sense of a deeply and completely motivated, consciously artistic interweaving of elements serious and pleasurable, of responsibility and play."

Whatever its roots in Africa, among black Americans, "cool" signified a certain elegant restraint, a control of facial expression, posture, and gesture, that projected danger as well as grace. Behind this outer calm, rivers of deep emotion and passion might be felt, but the exterior projected a laid-back hardness that intimidated men and seduced women. Jazz trumpeter Miles Davis gave musical expression to this ethos with his exquisite suits, red sports car, and musical mastery. With the 1957 release of his album *Birth of the Cool*, he became the poster child for cool.

Cool wasn't limited to black folks. (White movie idol Steve McQueen definitely possessed the required chill.) Nor could every black person achieve it. For many black big-city brothers, cool was an elusive prize. In their strident attempts to achieve cool, many became self-conscious parodies of the persona. Trying too hard to be cool was not cool. Cool was a way of being, not a goal to achieve. You were cool when others perceived you as such. It was not something you could declare yourself. Truly cool people are anointed by those around them and baptized by the appreciation of others.

Don remembered overhearing two girls in high school talking: "'You know, Don Cornelius thinks he's cool, doesn't he?' And the other girl said, 'No, honey. He is cool.' That's just something, for whatever it's worth and for whatever it means, that's something that's just born in me."

In the Chicago of his young manhood, cool was a currency that drew people to you, garnered respect, and made upward mobility easier. Cornelius's cool would help him impress authority figures, whether they were advertising executives, radio station personnel, or record-business gatekeepers. Cool was the intangible element in Don's rise that would be much commented on in later years but, in this early part of his career, it was the unspoken element that gave others confidence in him.

Now, to understand the heritage of WVON and why it was such a crucial stop in Cornelius's journey, we have to go back to the post–World War II period when, for the first time, black radio announcers with ethnic voices began appearing on the nation's airwaves. Black announcers had been on the radio before the war, but usually they'd been instructed to lose any black accent and cleanse their vocabulary of slang.

Arthur Bernard Leaner, aka Al Benson, a onetime vaudeville performer and sometime storefront preacher from Jackson, Mississippi, would break the mold and, in a number of ways, set the stage for *Soul*

Train. At the time, there were no stations dedicated to serving black listeners in the Chicago market. (In 1947, Memphis's WDIA became the first "negro"-oriented station; in 1949 the first to be black owned, WERD, opened in Atlanta.)

When Arthur debuted in Chicago radio in 1945, he hosted a fifteen-minute Sunday-night show during which he preached the gospel while a choir sang in the background. He'd expected to get underwriting from local advertisers, but a dispute with station management led Arthur to revamp his persona. Out went the preaching and the choir. In its place he became Al Benson, "the Ole Swingmaster," and he began playing blues, swing, and the emerging style of dance music eventually labeled rhythm and blues. By 1947 he was broadcasting twenty hours a week on two different stations and garnering advertising support from businesses around the city.

By 1948 the *Chicago Tribune* had declared Benson the most popular disc jockey in Chicago, white or black. Key to Benson's popularity was what he called "native talk," meaning that on the air he spoke with a southern black accent, used current slang, and referred to the struggles black immigrants from the South were confronting in the Windy City. By playing electrified urban blues or rhythm and blues, sounds then being released exclusively by independent labels like Chicago's Chess, Benson established a template for how black DJs could compete with their white counterparts and, eventually, for the sound and style of black radio that continued into the soul era and endures today in hip-hop radio.

With radio as his power base, Benson staged shows at the Regal Theater, Chicago's answer to New York's Apollo, and he started his own record label, Parrot Records. In 1951, a year before the debut of *American Bandstand*, Benson hosted his own variety show on a local station, making him the first black DJ in Chicago to do so (perhaps the first in the country). So Don Cornelius grew up with Al Benson as a huge, innovative figure in his world.

Benson's business acumen was very much in keeping with the energy of black Chicago, which, more than any other American metropolis, was home to some of the most important black businesses of the postwar era. John H. Sengstacke's weekly *Chicago Defender* was a force championing civil rights and the integration of the armed forces and encouraging southern blacks to move North. John Johnson founded *Ebony*, a monthly black version of *Life* magazine, in 1945 and followed up with the pocket-size *Jet* in 1951, both of which remain staples in black households. Black hair-care companies based in the city prospered as well, with Fred Luster's Luster Products, founded in 1957, and George Johnson's Johnson Products, started in 1954, both generating millions in profits and thousands of jobs in factories and beauty salons nationwide. And Chicagoan S. B. Fuller was one of the slickest black businessmen ever. He started selling products for a white company—soap and deodorant—door to door to South Side blacks in the 1920s. By 1939 he'd made enough money to open his own factory, and almost ten years later Fuller purchased the company of his white distributor (while wisely keeping his black identity secret). During the 1950s Fuller was likely the richest black man in America.

It was in this context that WVON, which arrived on air in 1963, made an immediate impact by serving as an outlet for black entrepreneurs to advertise products to a growing consumer market using an on-air delivery and music that Benson pioneered. The station was owned by Leonard and Phil Chess, two Polish brothers who ran Chess and Checker Records, home of Chuck Berry, Muddy Waters, Howlin' Wolf, Etta James, and countless other legends. While WVON's location at the far end of the AM dial and tiny 250-watt signal meant it couldn't be heard all over the city, the station still squarely hit its target—the city's densely packed black neighborhoods in South and West Side Chicago.

Though the radio scene had changed considerably since Al Benson's heyday, his stamp was still felt at WVON. He had sponsored contests for prospective DJs around the city and gave them airtime, inaugurating many of their careers, including those of Sid McCoy (who'd later be the voice of *Soul Train*) and Herb "the Cool Gent" Kent.

By the time Cornelius reached WVON in 1966, Benson was no longer a force, although he thrived through the voices of on-air personalities Kent, Pervis "the Blues Man" Spann, Wesley South, and news director Roy Wood, who guided the station's civil rights coverage. WVON's playlist was filled with music made in the city itself. Blues stars like Muddy Waters and Howlin' Wolf were starting to lose their hold on black listeners, but an exciting generation of local soul singers led by singer-songwriter Curtis Mayfield and including Jerry Butler, the Impressions, Gene Chandler, Fontella Bass, and Tyrone Davis were starting to deliver consistent hits and strong ratings.

Given the station's pedigree and power, it's not surprising that Don never landed a regular on-air slot playing music. Instead he was given the job of news reader and street reporter during one of the most tumultuous periods in Chicago history. In January 1966, Dr. Martin Luther King Jr. relocated to a Chicago housing project to dramatize the de facto segregation in real estate practices in the "liberal" North. King would face resistance from political boss Mayor Richard Daley, be confounded by nefarious dealings with black elected officials who were puppets of the local Democratic machine, and endure brutal harassment from Chicago's white residents during public marches. A photograph from this period shows a young Don with microphone in hand, covering the civil rights movement for WVON, walking down a Chicago street with King.

Don also covered the riots in the wake of King's assassination in April 4, 1968, and the violent events of that June's Democratic Convention that left demonstrators bloody in the city's streets. The Black Panthers organized successfully in Chicago under the leadership of

Fred Hampton, who was then murdered in a one-sided shoot-out with the city's police, another story Cornelius and WVON reported.

During this intense period in Chicago's history, Cornelius made his television debut, hosting a show on local UHF station WCIU called *A Black View of the News*, just one of scores of public-interest shows that were popping up around the country in response to the civil rights movement. Most had names as on the nose as the one Cornelius hosted, names that unintentionally suggested that "the black view" remained not merely segregated but exotic, even foreign, to the American mainstream.

Today the UHF broadcast band is used primarily for mobile phones and two-way radio. But in the 1960s UHF stations, which broadcast on a higher frequency than the standard VHF stations of commercial TV, were an alternative viewing experience. The signals had limited coverage and performed as a precursor to public-access TV years before cable's introduction. And this relationship with WCIU, initially based on Cornelius's news experience, led to the birth of *Soul Train*. The idea of doing a dance show was far from original. Aside from Dick Clark's *American Bandstand*, which aired nationally on ABC, there were local dance shows all around the country that catered to teenagers and, to varying degrees, included black singers and dancers. Almost none of the shows I'm aware of from the period placed soul, or "black music," so front and center: most of them used teen appeal to keep local advertisers and TV programmers comfortable. Don's genius was seeing that the time was right for a more explicitly "soul"—that is, black—show.

The *Soul Train* name goes back to Don's tenure at WVON. Air personnel at radio stations supplemented their income by hosting parties with recording artists at local clubs or schools. Depending on the venue, these were either dance parties or sock hops. Record labels would provide acts free of charge for the DJs' appearances, which served as an inducement for them to play the acts' music on air.

Cornelius did mostly news, so he partnered up with another young WVON personality, DJ Joe Carr, to promote his events. "We'd take relatively small shows to various schools and play shows in the school auditorium and then pack up real quick and take it to another auditorium," Don said. "It just felt like a train to me moving around the city, and I think I called it 'Soul Train.' So when I got the green light at channel twenty-six to do my version of a new dance show, I automatically called it *Soul Train*."

"People look at *Soul Train* on its surface and assume that it was a tremendous challenge," Cornelius said of first presenting the idea. "That it was real hard, and it was almost impossible, and you almost had to kill somebody, but it wasn't. It wasn't any of that. Television again is a medium where if you come up with a good enough idea, it just goes right on. It just steps right up, it just happens, and you can always find necessary support if the idea is strong enough, and *Soul Train* was apparently a very strong idea. I will never forget. I had a friend who was an executive at Sears. He knew me as a guy who was always trying to come up with an idea to do this or that, and he humored me a lot. And so when I came up with this *Soul Train* idea, I made my way into his office. Sears executives on his level had cubicles, and they could even see you coming through the glass, and so George O'Hare was working the phones as usual. I came and sat down next to him, and he gave me one of these looks like, you know, You again, huh? And I just leaned over to his ear and said, 'George. *Soul Train*.' And the guy looked over to his secretary and said, 'Hold my calls.' So we knew immediately that that was an idea that had tremendous merit."

Cornelius approached WCUI with Sears, Roebuck as a sponsor. Not only did the station agree to broadcast the show, but it didn't ask for a piece of the pie. He was "fully open to them saying, 'You do this here, but we're gonna own it.' I was fully open to that, but they didn't say that. By the time someone made mention of the possibility of the station owning the show, I had already licensed it. So it was an accident. I would like to say I'm just a genius. But it just happened. If they had said, 'Sign here and this belongs to us,' I would've said, 'No problem,' but they didn't say it."

WCUI had studios in the beautiful Board of Trade Building, an art deco masterwork at the intersection of West Jackson and LaSalle. The building, which opened in 1930, is known to moviegoers for its prominent roles in *Ferris Bueller's Day Off* and *The Untouchables*, and as the home of Wayne Enterprises in Christopher Nolan's Batman films. The station was using studios in the building to air the daily seven-hour show *Stock Market Observer*, a testament to the import of grain in the Midwest.

The station had a tiny studio on the forty-third floor, which actually had already been the site of two previous dance shows—*Kiddie a-Go-Go* in 1966 and *Red Hot and Blues* in 1967—prior to *Soul Train*'s debut on August 17, 1970. The headliners were established Chicago soul star Jerry Butler and the local vocal group the Chi-Lites, who were about to embark on a string of hits in the early 1970s.

The set was not exactly state of the art. "It had a very local look to it," Don later recalled ruefully. "It was very small studio. We didn't have color cameras. We weren't able to play back very much because the station didn't have videotape cameras. That's the reason why we don't have archival footage."

Fawn Quinones, one of the original dancers on the Chicago show (who years later would appear on the LA broadcasts), said, "After hearing it advertised, I got on an L and went across town to the Board of Trade Building . . . So when I showed up I was wondering where was all the people. Well, I was the people."

Fawn remembers Don wearing a giant Afro and a maxi coat and being "so funny."

Gladys Knight & the Pips, best known for their soulful hits including "I Heard It Through the Grapevine" and "Midnight Train to Georgia," were early supporters of *Soul Train*.

"They had about fifty kids in there, and they had one camera, and we were in this little room and everyone was sweating to beat the band" is how O'Jays lead singer Eddie Levert recalls the Board of Trade studio. "We did not at the time know that it was going to catch on like it did. But it was an opportunity for black kids in the ghetto to get a chance to do their little dancing and to have their exposure."

His longtime partner in the O'Jays, Walter Williams, said, "It looked huge when you saw it on the screen, and everyone was having an absolute ball. This could be big if it goes further than local."

Soul Train's potential was obvious to the O'Jays. "It was just hard to get on a show like *American Bandstand* because you had this large influx of white artists before you," said Levert, "people like Jan and Dean, and all of the sudden you felt like a sore thumb in there. You look around and you're surrounded by all this beach music and we're coming to do R&B."

Williams chimed in: "[To get on] *American Bandstand*, and *Hullabaloo* and *Shindig*, you had to have a hit record. You had to have a Top 40 record, and most R&B was not crossing over to that magnitude, and that's probably why we were not invited to those kinds of shows. Don's show, if you had an R&B hit, you were automatically in the mix."

"There was an automatic connection because he was struggling to get his foot in the door like *American Bandstand*," said Levert. "He was struggling to become a mainstay, and we were still struggling trying to become a hit act. So our purposes are the same. Our relationship became one such as people who were trying to explore and try to get the next level. And automatically [we] became comrades and friends."

This connection between Don and the O'Jays—who in 1970 were on the verge of their star-making run of Sound of Philadelphia hits—would be ongoing. Following this first appearance on the original *Soul Train*, the vocal trio would, between Chicago and Los Angeles, do the show thirteen times over the decades.

Michelle Garner, a Chicago native and later an advertising executive who would work with *Soul Train*, remembers seeing the Chicago show. "It was on like five days a week," Garner said, "so the kids would come home from school. It's kind of like appointment TV, and they're all excited about it. It was certainly after we had just come off the riots, after the death of Martin Luther King, so you know it's kind of like in rebuilding mode. Everything was trying to get back in a nice calm state . . . Before that, all we had were stage shows. That's the only time you would see the acts when they would go the Regal Theater and see all the acts for two dollars or whatever. So to see them on television just added a whole dynamic."

Many of the *Soul Train* staples that became famous began as accompaniment to the Chicago show. Sid McCoy's dulcet tone, which was even deeper and smoother than Don's, had introduced the show from the very start. To Don he "was the greatest disc jockey that the city of Chicago has ever known" and "one of my heroes."

The screaming "*Soooooooooouuuuulllll Train!*" voice that has been imitated for generations is the voice of Don's WVON colleague Joe Carr. Don was playing around in the studio, trying to create a commercial break for the show, when Carr stuck his head into the booth and, in a playful mood, did his thing. "That's it," Don said. "That's what I'm looking for, and for the whole three decades we never took his voice off the *Soul Train* show."

Just as enduring, both beloved and disparaged, was the scramble board, which had the names of soul singers, politicians, and historical figures hidden amid a wall of jumbled letters. Though never designed to tax the minds of its young contestants, it was always amusing to see how long it took folks to figure out the obvious. "We needed a feature something like [*American Bandstand*'s] Rate a Record, but not quite as stupid, and we deemed the scramble board as being not quite as stupid, but stupid" was Don's unsentimental recollection of the feature's genesis. "Over the years people came to me and said, 'Well, when are you going to change that scramble board and get rid of the scramble board?' And I would always say, '*Bandstand* never got rid of Rate a Record, so why do we have to get rid of scramble board?' Because it is just as stupid. You're following what I'm saying? So that's why it's always been with us. Because it was never intended to be a stroke of genius of any kind. It was just intended to give kids a chance to stand up by the scramble board."

In his interview for the VH1 doc, Don said the original *Soul Train* theme was a song called "Hot Potatoes," and I think it was by a guy named Eddie Robinson." Memory failed the TV host on this one. The original version of the song was recorded in 1963 by the soul saxophone giant King Curtis, backed by a band called the Rimshots, which may be where Don's recollection of "Eddie Robinson" comes from.

The *Soul Train* scramble board was one of the show's most popular staples.

Tragically, King Curtis was stabbed to death outside his home in Harlem in 1971, the same year *Soul Train* would go national. Enjoy Records, the New York indie label that had the rights to the record, renamed the track "Soul Train (Parts 1 & 2)" and the band the Rimshots, removing King Curtis's name from the single.

Whatever the song was called, it was a funky instrumental with Curtis's wailing tenor sax, a dark, sexy organ, and a laid-back groove suggesting an after-hours gathering at a smoky South Side bar. It was the kind of funky jazz performance that was typical in the early to mid-1960s when Don was spinning part-time at WVON. Eventually it would be replaced by something more memorable.

Don's catalog of on-air DJ slang is legendary, most of it either refinements of catchphrases from other WVON DJs, Chicago street slang, or phrases of his own invention. For example, "You can bet your last money, it's all gonna be a stone gas, honey" is definitely an R&B radio catchphrase, something usually said to promote a party or a show at the

Regal. His signature show closer "As always in parting we wish you—love, peace, and *soul*!" is not unlike the closing rhymes many of the popular black DJs used, at WVON and elsewhere, to stamp their broadcasts. Drawing upon the rich tradition of black DJs, Don brought the casual cool and rhyming style of those on-air voices to broadcast television.

But without a doubt the signature symbol of *Soul Train* was the human alley that dancers moved through every week. Known as the *Soul Train* line and inspired by showy dances at house parties and clubs nationwide, this was a showcase for creativity, sexuality, and fun. It would be on the *Soul Train* line that careers were born, stars were showcased, and dynamic new directions in dance emerged. Its roots were quite humble. Don saw it done all the time at parties he attended around Chicago in the fifties and sixties. So it was no great brainstorm but a fun midwestern social ritual that, via television, became a bit of a national obsession.

"It was overnight hot," said Don about the show's impact in Chi-Town. "Overnight because of the fact that nothing was ever targeted at them. Nothing ever targeted us. When it came on it was like, almost in minutes, every black person in town knew about it, and not because it was a wonderful show but because it was theirs . . . They felt that was something on television that was designed to target our audience. Or my audience. The community has always been there for us and has always treated *Soul Train* like it belonged to them."

As a teenager living in Gary, Indiana, Reggie Thornton would come up for Thursday tapings of the show, making the trip on the South Shore train that he says was subsidized by Cornelius. "Then all of a sudden Don Cornelius got an idea to make a pilot for *Soul Train* and to bring it out here to California, to make it a nationwide show," says Thornton. "I didn't know what a pilot was, but Don Cornelius called my parents and asked could he get permission to use me in a pilot for *Soul Train*. I knew that I was going to be on national television once this pilot took off."

The show was such an immediate local success that black hair-care giant Johnson Products reached out and expressed interest in syndicating it nationally. The Afro was in full bloom, and the company's Afro Sheen product was one of the most popular ways to keep your 'fro soft and round. Its owner and founder, George Johnson, inspired by the new opportunities for black business, was in an expansive mood. During this same year, he was in the process of founding the Independence Bank and getting his company on the American Stock Exchange, making Johnson Products the first African American–owned company to make the cut. According to some of Don's business associates, Johnson agreed to put up $600,000 to fund the show if it was national. Johnson was hoping for a slot on one of the three major networks, but CBS, NBC, and ABC all turned the show down.

So Cornelius and Johnson went the syndication route, looking to the many independent stations around the country that were constantly searching for ways to carve out a niche audience in competition with the networks. In cities like New York and Chicago, there was a lot of after-school programming aimed at schoolkids (cartoon shows hosted by genial, goofy adults and talking puppets) and late-night black-and-white movies. Not unlike the landscape during the early days of radio, many of the shows on local stations had a major advertiser who would underwrite the broadcast.

Johnson Products and Don initially hoped to expand the show to twenty-four cities, but the response was tepid, with only seven cities (Atlanta, Cleveland, Detroit, Houston, San Francisco, and, crucially, Philadelphia and Los Angeles) ordering episodes.

But could *Soul Train* stay in Chicago and succeed? "We had our experience in Chicago, and when we decided to grow the show into something more sophisticated, we realized very early on that the kind of production talent and experience that we would require was not in Chicago," Don said. "At the same time, we realized that that kind of experience and skill in terms of personnel were falling all over themselves in Los Angeles looking for work . . . If you wanted to do *Soul Train* in a bigger way, you had to go to LA."

Los Angeles had long been the promised land for anyone enamored of a show-business career. That's where all the movie studios and television networks were based, and a number of the major record labels had significant operations there. Los Angeles had already claimed another Chi-Town pop culture institution: Hugh Hefner's *Playboy* had shifted many of its operations to the West Coast for these same reasons.

But for black people, LA wouldn't have been as attractive without Motown's example. Berry Gordy's pioneering record company had made surprising inroads on network TV, coproducing a number-one-rated NBC special (1968's *TCB*, also known as *Taking Care of Business with Diana Ross & the Supremes and the Temptations*), making alliances with big talent agencies, and carefully moving the record company west between 1968 and 1971. The Jackson Five, though signed in Detroit, would be relocated to Los Angeles and would, in clothing style and positioning, reflect the sun-kissed Hollywood environment.

Motown's move to LA would ignite a historic shift in black entertainment. Starting in the 1970s, LA would become the de facto headquarters for popular black music. Motown moved to a building on Sunset Boulevard, and scores of artists, producers, and industry professionals from Detroit, Memphis, New York, Philadelphia, and Chicago moved west as the major record labels were, influenced by Motown's success, investing heavily in black music. All the LA-based labels (MCA, Warner Bros., Capitol), as well as those in New York, inaugurated black music departments, expanding their rosters of artists and staff and raising the value of recording contracts and, increasingly, salaries in the field.

A kind of media civil rights movement, a delayed reaction to the real civil rights movement, was under way, which led previously reluctant mainstream businesses to distribute black content and banks to invest in products aimed at black consumers. The 1960s had been a time of marching and protests, political activities that opened doors for black advancement that had never before existed in the United States. For many, the 1970s would be a time to capitalize on these new opportunities. A popular phrase at the time was "black capitalism" (though President Richard Nixon's use of the term made many question its value). Publications aimed at upscale black audiences (*Essence* and *Black Enterprise*) were founded, and FM stations that featured soul and funk artists debuted in New York, Philadelphia, Washington, DC, and other major markets—many of them black owned.

Blaxploitation movies, driven by dynamic soundtracks composed by Isaac Hayes, Curtis Mayfield, Marvin Gaye, James Brown, Willie Hutch, and others made box-office noise while creating a stable of sepia movie stars. A new generation of black record labels, led by Kenny Gamble and Leon Huff's prolific Philadelphia International Records, were having massive pop hits. Don Cornelius's weekly show would be part of this shift, but not while it was based out of a small studio in a Chicago business building.

Soul Train's move to LA didn't mean abandoning Chi-Town. For a while Don traveled between the two cities, continuing to host the local Chicago version while launching the national show. Even after stopping that killer schedule, the Chicago show was broadcast throughout the seventies with Don's associate Clinton Ghent hosting. Don would, in manner and style, remain a Chicagoan the rest of his life. One of the subtexts of moving *Soul Train* to LA would be his own sometimes-humorous adjustment to life in the City of Angels.

One overarching theme of *Soul Train* in Chicago that set the stage for the show's future was Don's ability to build alliances. Just as the radio innovator Al Benson had formed strong ties between himself and the various radio stations and advertisers of postwar Chicago, Cornelius built partnerships with talent (the O'Jays, Jerry Butler) and business folks (George Johnson) at the tail end of the civil rights movement that would sustain him and his enterprise for years.

Chapter 2
LOVE, PEACE, AND SOUL

||||||||||||||||||||||||||||||||||||||

ON AUGUST 11, 1965, Marquette Frye, a young black man in his twenties, was pulled over in the Watts section of Los Angeles by a California Highway Patrolman on suspicion of driving drunk. Marquette told the officer he wasn't intoxicated, and an argument began. Marquette's brother Ronald, who'd been in the car, ran to get his mother from their nearby home. The patrolman called for backup. As the Frye family argued with police, a growing crowd of the family's predominantly black neighbors gathered to protest what they deemed police harassment. Locals tossed bottles at the police. The entire Frye family was arrested. More police arrived on the scene. So did more angry Watts residents.

Years of tension between the police and the black population came to a head that August night in 1965. Led by Chief of Police William Parker, the LAPD had recruited southern-born whites and developed a militarized, confrontational philosophy toward young black men that was a motorized version of the twenty-first century's stop-and-frisk. Parker encouraged police authorities in Los Angeles, whether the LAPD, the CHP (California Highway Patrol), or members of the sheriff's department, to err on the side of suspicion and intimidation in any interaction with young black males.

Though segregation was not officially on the books in LA, the city's residency laws were full of "covenants" that restricted sales of homes in desirable areas to blacks, Hispanics, or Asians, forcing them to live primarily in East LA, Compton, South LA, and Watts. This is the backdrop for six days of fighting, shooting, and burning that would result in thirty-four deaths, the deployment of 3,900 national guardsmen, and $40 million in property damage. The 1960s would see race riots break out in many big cities around the United States, most triggered by a similarly combustible mix of aggressive policing and black resentment. But few were as brutal as the Watts riots in Los Angeles in 1965.

Many of the thousands who participated in the Watts rebellion shouted "Burn, baby, burn!"—a slogan used by local DJ the Magnificent Montague to hype a hot record he was spinning and, like much soul radio slang, also a sexual double entendre. However, in the riot's wake, Montague was accused by LA mayor Sam Yorty of inciting local blacks to riot with his phrase "Burn, baby, burn!" In the sixties there were many urban riots and many serious-minded official reports issued in their aftermath. Watts was no exception. A former CIA director was called in and would issue a report outlining all of the racial and institutional reasons for the riots. But as was typical of the time, the report's recommendations for change were resoundingly ignored by LA's city fathers: issues with the police were brushed aside (later igniting the 1992 riots), and restrictive real estate policies took decades to loosen. However, a few positive things came out of the immediate official reaction. Just two years after the Watts riots, Alain Leroy Locke High

School, named after the Harlem Renaissance poet, was opened at 325 East 111th Street in Watts. The school was clearly a peace offering to a community that was overpoliced and underserved. While the school did not make the neighborhood any safer or the policing any less intrusive, it did become a magnet for talented young people seeking a career in music. Locke High School would go on to nurture several generations of top musicians, including smooth jazz saxophonist Gerald Albright, drummer Leon "Ndugu" Chancler (who'd play on Michael Jackson's "Billie Jean"), vocalist-actor Tyrese Gibson (a staple of the *Fast & Furious* franchise), and pianist-vocalist Patrice Rushen.

Rushen was a petite, precocious talent who'd become one of Locke's most beloved musicians, evolving from a teenage keyboard prodigy into a singer and recording artist with the signature eighties hits "Remind Me" and "Forget Me Nots" (both of which would be widely sampled on rap records in the nineties). It was during her tenure at Locke that she became part of the first class of *Soul Train* dancers.

Rushen: The community that surrounded Locke was right in the thick of where the riots had been, and there was a concerted effort to build that community back. It had always been close-knit, and the riots blew it apart. So in bringing it back together, the music department kept the kids busy and involving us in activities that would allow us to see beyond just where we lived. I think it was very important. So being a member of the largest gang going, when you're in the band, there's 250 of you. Carrying an instrument case was a big deal. People didn't mess with us. They really were proud of the fact that we worked hard and we learned a lot, and between Locke's band and the drill team, we became nationally known.

Patrice Rushen danced on the show as a teen and returned years later as a performer.

In 1971 Don Cornelius came over to Locke and visited the
school's summer program to talk about "this special show that they
were gonna start, and it was a dance show, and it was going to feature R&B artists primarily," Rushen said. "They wanted kids from
the community to participate, to come out. Sounded good to me. I
was already into music, very, very heavily, music of all kinds, and an
opportunity to be on television was right up my alley, and so I decided
to tell a few friends and said, Let's go down there. They brought a
bus. We loaded into a bus and they took us over to KTTV and we
went into the studio and we said, 'Well, what do we do?' He said,
'Just enjoy yourselves. Dance to the music and have a great time.'
And that's what we did." Rushen and her friends participated in the
recording of eight *Soul Train*s that first year in LA.

> **Cornelius:** I was just looking for people who look well. Who
> look good on camera and who could dance well. That's all I was
> looking for, and once we got out here we realized that the LA
> youth, the Los Angeles population, was much more than that.
> They were exciting to look at. Just plain exciting to look at . . .
> They had the bodies, the facial features, the hair, the movement.
> They had stuff you just didn't find much. Where I came from,
> people who looked that good, they didn't want to be on TV. It was
> people who probably shouldn't be on TV wanted to be on TV, but
> when we hit LA it was all those people that should be on TV, had
> wanted to be on TV. There was just so much glamour. So much
> invention, so much creativity.

What's interesting about this effusive praise for California dancers is that this is very much hindsight talking. As we'll see, Don's
initial feelings about dancing out West were very different.

Locke High would be one of the three local institutions that would feed dancers to *Soul Train* in the key first two seasons after the show had relocated to Los Angeles. The other two were Denker Park in South Central and Maverick's Flat nightclub on Crenshaw Boulevard were also crucial, playing different, though parallel, roles. Locke brought Don into contact with a new important educational institution and blossoming talent like Rushen, who would not only dance on early shows but would come back years later to perform on it. The future hit maker has strong memories of the fifth *Soul Train* episode, during which she was able to ask questions of singer-songwriters Bill Withers and Al Green. Reflecting on her career, Rushen thinks that early music-business exposure definitely "filtered into my musicianship."

Rushen: Because we were taping the shows, there were stops and starts, and for me that was golden time, because during the stops is when I could really keep my eyes on the artists, and, you know, go up to them. There were no barriers. Nobody would say, Don't speak to them, don't do this, don't do that. We were all there together taping. So you could actually talk to people, and you would get some good feedback sometimes. And bits and pieces of information that as a musician—even though I was on the show dancing—as a musician were very helpful, and then watching people perform. Watching that moment that happens when they're not on, and that split second of immediate change that comes together when then they're on. That was like a golden opportunity for me to be up close and see that.

The next venue for recruitment was the Denker Recreation Center, located at 1550 West Thirty-fifth Place between two major avenues, Western and Normandie. It was a multipurpose facility with a baseball field and an indoor gym, but Denker's biggest asset wasn't the facility itself—it was city recreation director Pam Brown, who'd been with the city since 1964 and had shifted to Denker in '69. Brown had a previous brush with show business when she helped recruit kids for a taping of Ralph Edwards's popular *This Is Your Life* TV series. It was through this connection that she met Don Cornelius.

"When I first met Don and he came to one of the parks where the young people were to audition, he said, 'California kids. These LA kids don't know how to dance.' He was real cool with it, and I said, 'Well, you don't know. You've got something in store when you watch them dance, because they can be very creative.'" That audition, actually held at nearby Queens Park, attracted about seventy-five kids. "Don said, 'Okay. They're all right.' It was hard to get something constructive out of Don. You always had to work a little harder."

Brown traveled to predominantly black schools all over LA, including Locke, Dorsey, Freemont, and Bret Harte Junior High. Another audition at Denker was incredibly well attended, drawing more than four hundred wannabes. "There wasn't any room in the gymnasium because so many had come. Don says 'Okay, we're on it now. We're on it.'" Still, the initial taping of *Soul Train*, headlined by Gladys Knight & the Pips and ex-Temptation Eddie Kendricks, had, by Brown's account, only about thirty dancers.

The third and, ultimately, most important feeder of dancers to the show was Maverick's Flat, located at 4225 Crenshaw Boulevard, which was the alpha and omega of the city's black entertainment world. Owned by local businessman, musician, and actor John Daniels, Maverick's Flat opened in 1966, in the wake of the Watts riots, with the purpose of providing an entertainment center for folks who didn't want to travel up to Hollywood for fun. The club, just down the hill from middle- and upper-class black home owners in

Baldwin Hills, View Park, and Ladera Heights, was by 1971 billing itself as "the Apollo Theater of Los Angeles," and for a long time it lived up to that billing, attracting everyone who was anyone in the world of R&B/funk, black comedy, and movies. Testament to its popularity is that the Temptations' *Psychedelic Shack* LP cover was influenced by the Playboy Club by way of the drug-den decor of Maverick's Flat. Daniels was quite a flamboyant character, a muscular, big-Afroed man who starred in *Black Shampoo*, a bad 1976 remake of the critically acclaimed Warren Beatty vehicle about a sex-machine LA hairdresser.

Earth, Wind & Fire, the Commodores, the Whispers, and Lakeside were among the bands to perform there regularly. Howard Hewett, future lead singer of Shalamar, was in Maverick's Flat's house band. Richard Pryor often worked out his routines there, and all of black Hollywood's newly minted movie stars (Jim Brown, Pam Grier, Fred Williamson) came through. Its slogan "Where it's at? Maverick's Flat" was LA seventies slang for the club being an in-crowd destination.

Almost every one of the Los Angeles–based dancers who starred on *Soul Train* in its 1970s peak went there to dance. Dancer-performer Jeffrey Daniel recalls his early trips to Maverick's Flat. "You have to understand," he said, "as great as the show was and as great as the dancing was, what you see on *Soul Train* is about a quarter of what they do if you see them in clubs. *Soul Train* is very controlled. It's like, 'Okay, sit down. Okay, now dance.' . . . When you're in the club, it's freestyle."

So as Don settled into LA, seeing teenagers from Locke and Denker and older movers from Maverick's Flat, he had to adjust his taste in dancing.

Cornelius: When I first saw how the kids in LA danced, it was a little wild and crazy for me because I was from the cool school in

Chicago. The kids in LA were like throwing it at you . . . When I got here, I couldn't feel it. I couldn't feel it. I couldn't handle it. It was only after the show became successful that I realized what a great thing these kids brought to television. If you had given me a choice, I would have said to all of them, Please don't dance like that. It's nasty, okay? It's not cool. That's what I would have said. But the television audience disagreed.

During *Soul Train*'s first season in LA, only twenty-eight shows were taped (as opposed to thirty-nine and thirty-seven in the following seasons). The show had to prove itself—to TV stations, major acts, and the record industry. The dancing would be essential because a look at the talent during that 1971–72 season shows an overabundance of acts from Chicago. Ten of that season's shows featured Chicago-based or -born talent, with singer Lou Rawls appearing twice. Clearly Don was leaning on his hometown contacts.

Al Bell, then president of Stax Records, was ambitious, highly political, and a proud black nationalist and major supporter of the show. Almost every major act on the Stax roster except Isaac Hayes would soon perform on *Soul Train*: Rufus Thomas, Carla Thomas, the Staple Singers, the Bar-Kays, the Emotions, Luther Ingram. This grew out of a concert Bell organized in 1972 at the massive Los Angeles Coliseum with virtually every act on his roster. Tickets were only a dollar. Reverend Jesse Jackson led the crowd in a roaring chant of a poem called "I Am Somebody." While it obviously promoted the Stax label, the event also attempted to provide moral and spiritual support to LA's black community. So it was no surprise that Bell would make his acts available to TV's first national black music show.

Motown Records, who'd just come west themselves, provided a number of performers as well (Junior Walker, Edwin Starr, the Originals), but none of its biggest names (Diana Ross, the Temptations, the Four Tops, Stevie Wonder). Berry Gordy's empire, though supportive of the show, took a bit of a wait-and-see approach to *Soul Train* when it came to its marquee talent.

While the industry was being introduced to *Soul Train*, Cornelius was establishing some enduring production habits. The animation of the opening-title graphics and the rumbling soulful train would be a staple of the show, while always being updated, as would the stage itself. Originally the *Soul Train* intro featured stick-figure animation with the names of the stations airing the show as slates on the train tracks. In addition, there was a circular railroad sign and a caution strip across the stage. As the show added more stations, the lights became neon and had flashing wheels. During the disco years, the obligatory light-reflecting disco ball was added, with SOUL TRAIN lined up around it. At one time, the stage was glass. Another version had flashing wheels and lights in front that backlit the *Soul Train* line.

For the majority of *Soul Train*'s history, the animation for the opening, as well as the bumpers, was done by a man named John Cole, who took the train from dancing on its hind legs to puffing smoke to shooting fire as it passed through a cityscape. Though most people saw the show on Saturday mornings, a number of fans report being scared by the animation as children, that despite the great music that opening would lead them to, it also created great unease.

Cornelius wrote all the scripts that first year and would write them right through 2006. "No one really understands how many hours he put in writing the show," said his son Tony, who watched his father work. "Obviously, when he hosted the show for years, people would listen to the dialogue and think, That's the same dialogue I heard last week. But he really put in a lot of time to make sure he did his research on these artists. He knew exactly who they were, he knew exactly what songs they were going to perform, and he tried to get into their soul, but he got into their soul his way. People don't realize how difficult it is to write scripts and think about questions to ask artists who may or may not be prepared for certain questions. He really went beyond the call of duty to take it upon himself to sit down every night and write scripts for almost thirty years or more."

The *Soul Train* scripts, like the show itself, were an extension of Don's career in black radio. They deftly captured the slang and flavor of the radio disc jockey and were filled with enough catchphrases to fill an MC's rhyme book. Just as idiosyncratic as the scripts was Don's interview style. Comic Cedric the Entertainer, who grew up watching the show in Missouri, had a humorous take on it. "I realized it had to be his show because his interview skills was one that I could not easily understand," he recalled. "I mean, 'cause he never really asked a question. He was the only person I knew that made statements and, you know, posed them as questions. 'So you're on tour?' Pause. 'Yes, I am on tour.' 'The album is selling.' Pause. 'Yes, it's selling.' You know that was Don's style. But he was smooth with it."

For Fab 5 Freddy Brathwaite, the future *Yo! MTV Raps* host who watched the show growing up in Brooklyn, Cornelius's interview style was defined by his height. "He's taller than everybody he's probably interviewed," said Brathwaite. "He had such a cool and commanding presence. Literally the epitome. Nothing ever cooler on TV except for maybe if a James Bond movie was playing. When I think of Don's interview style, he didn't say a lot. He asked a couple of key questions, let you get your thing off, and that was it. His demeanor was the essence of cool."

Cornelius's relationship with the dancers, with a few warmhearted exceptions we'll get into later, remained the same for the show's more than one thousand episodes. "Don Cornelius was like a dad sitting in the room over in the corner," said dancer Derek Fleming. "He didn't have a lot of time for you. He was very stern, very focused, and I wouldn't say cold, but he was at work, and you had to be careful how you crossed him while he was at work."

But, especially in *Soul Train*'s early years, his words were appetizers, and the dancers were the main course.

THE DANCING was the alpha and omega of the *Soul Train* story. It is more important than Don Cornelius's slang, the scramble board, and even the stars gracing its stage. The show's impact on dance starts from a very basic fact of black life: "Around the time we started *Soul Train*, wherever you would go in the United States, there was a different style of dancing," Don said. "You would go to Detroit and they would be doing one thing. You could go to Chicago, and it was real cool . . . And you would go down south to Atlanta, and there was a whole 'nother flavor."

I can cosign this. I remember many summer vacations going down to Virginia from Brooklyn, and my sister and I were grilled about the latest dances up north and forced to demonstrate until the steps had been passed on. Part of the appeal of James Brown's live show was that he, like an anthropologist of movement, had collected dances as he traveled, turning the Camel Walk into either a record or a piece of his impeccable show. Dick Clark's *Bandstand* certainly played its role in establishing many national dance trends (such as the 1960s phenomenon that was the twist). But the few black Philadelphia high school kids who got onto *American Bandstand* had a huge impact on what dances made it onto the broadcast. So while black dance style was included in Clark's broadcast, it was in small doses and often performed by white teens imitating their black peers. This kind of cultural co-optation was typical of American culture for most of this nation's history: black style—in music, dance, slang, and attitude—watered down for white mass consumption.

This is precisely why *Soul Train* was so revolutionary. This was black dance by black dancers presented by a black producer via a mass-media platform. This wasn't isolated exposure on a black radio station at the end of the AM dial, or a brief appearance by James Brown or Jackie Wilson on the *Ed Sullivan Show*. This was a regularly scheduled get-down right in your living room, whether you were black or white.

What viewers saw on *Soul Train* wasn't just one style but a polyglot of approaches, some indigenous street dance, some just individual flamboyance, and often happy accidents discovered in the heat of competition. From the show's national debut up to when break-dancing went pop in the 1980s, *Soul Train* was the most important showcase for contemporary idiomatic dance in the world. Music videos eventually usurped that role, but it didn't happen immediately. Most of the dancers' profiles to come are of folks from that golden era.

Never had the vernacular dances of black folks—dances that have roots in African religious rites and that traveled, by force and DNA, across the Atlantic Ocean—had such a vivid national showcase. Moves that in Africa would have had a connection to a god of water or fertility had been transformed into a model of self-expression unique to the American experience. There was an ecstatic nature to the best *Soul Train* dances. The writer Albert Murray, in writing about the blues, used the phrase "Saturday-night ritual" to explain the raucous parties that happened at juke joints of the South. With *Soul Train*, it was Saturday-morning celebrations.

"In the history of dance, *Soul Train* has its own place," said Debbie Allen, a choreographer, dancer, and actress with a highly distinguished show-business career: two Tony Awards, three Emmys, and a choreographer and star in TV's *Fame* series. So she knows dancing. "You know there are different generations and genres of dance that can never be duplicated but will always be imitated . . . And *Soul Train* has its own lane because it inspired millions and millions. Look how long it lasted, and look how many people went through that show . . . There's so many choreographers that you will never know that they honed their skills watching *Soul Train*."

Soul Train brought funky booty-shaking moves into America's living rooms.

The show was a Saturday ritual watched with religious fervor and dedication. Instead of putting a donation in the collection plate, you purchased Afro Sheen, read *Right On!* magazine, or simply imitated the dances you witnessed in an act of supplication. *Soul Train* wasn't explicitly church, though Don Cornelius would have been a spectacularly cool pastor. Yet there was a spiritual quality to the dancing in *Soul Train* that touched the soul of viewers. Damita Jo Freeman, Jeffrey Daniel, Fred Berry, Jody Watley, Tyrone Proctor, Lou Ski, Rosie Perez, and the scores of dancers who created the *Soul Train* tradition preached with their torsos, legs, and arms, speaking a human language that was as influential as any Sunday sermon.

DANCER PROFILE: Damita Jo and Don Campbell

If you Google Damita Jo Freeman, one of the first items to pop up is a YouTube clip called "The sensational and dynamic Damita Jo Freeman." It is a four-minute-twenty-second greatest-hits montage of the moves that years later earned her the title of *Soul Train*'s "Best Creative Dance." The clip starts with a taste of Damita Jo and several male partners grooving down the *Soul Train* line in four different episodes. Then it cuts to Freeman joining James Brown and the JB's during a driving version of "Super Bad." The Hardest-Working Man in Show Business is clearly fascinated by Damita Jo's smoothly robotic moves. The next cut is to a historic dance with Joe Tex, a jovial, energetic maker of gimmicky dance jams, performing his salacious 1972 hit "I Gotcha," with Freeman upstaging his lip-synched performance by gloriously pirouetting on her right leg. This clip encapsulates the *Soul Train* effect: well-known performer upstaged by an unknown dancer and loving it. Game recognizes game.

Unlike most of the dancers who defined *Soul Train*, Damita Jo was extremely well trained, having studied ballet in Los Angeles from ages eight to seventeen after her family moved west from St. Louis. Her ability to dance solidly, with her shoulders square, creating a straight up-and-down line while simultaneously balancing on one leg and snapping a limb out with panache, can be traced back to her classical training.

But that well-honed technique was in service to a fly, flamboyant sensibility that was as funky as an old bog of collard greens. Damita Jo's combination of precision and flair in popular dance is as rare now as it was then. No wonder the Godfather of Soul, himself one of the most influential dancers of all time, could barely take his eyes off her.

Love for Damita Jo was pervasive in black America. Freddie Jackson, one of the biggest R&B stars of the 1980s, speaks for many when he said, "Damita Jo used to teach. She used to give lessons. She used to give Saturday lessons. I don't think anybody kicked like her . . . She had moves. She had creativity. When you saw Damita Jo doing all that stuff, you used to see in clubs and watch people doing what Damita Jo Freeman had done that day on *Soul Train*. So I go back and say she was a teacher."

Echoing Jackson, Nieci Payne, a popular 1980s *Soul Train* dancer, proudly admitted Damita Jo's influence. "I mean, I had my own style of dance, but Damita Jo Freeman was everything dance-wise to me . . . Her look, her expression, everything. I just copied it and did it and won dances and danced all over the world with that. She's a good friend, a very good friend of mine to this day, and I tell everyone I danced on *Soul Train* because of Damita Jo Freeman."

Freeman's journey into dance history began on a Thursday night at Maverick's Flat when she and some girlfriends spotted a group of young men doing a dance she'd never seen. Don Campbell, Joe Chism, Jimmy "Scooby Doo" Foster, and some others were just starting to kick the tires on a dance soon to be famous internationally as "locking." "I thought it was the most magical thing I've ever seen," she told Stephen McMillian more than twenty years later. But it wasn't until the next night at Climax, another hot club, that Damita Jo got the courage to dance with the boys, make friends, and later bond over a postparty meal at Fat Burger.

What exactly did Freeman see those first two nights? Jeffrey Daniel, in a few years to be a big part of this scene, said with awe:

Don Campbell in the club? My God, why wasn't that filmed? Why wasn't that filmed? Taking off his hat, spinning it, putting it on his head. Throwing his car keys in the air, catching it in his hip pocket all to the beat of the music. Doing double splits, screaming, grabbing the ceiling, coming down a slap, and you could hear his hands slap the floor, these wooden floors, real dance floors. Just hear his hand. Pow! He just fills the whole club. I mean it was just amazing watching this guy.

Campbell, a street-dance innovator, the creator of locking and founder of the Lockers, was born in St. Louis in 1951 but raised in South Central. Drawing was his first artistic expression, and it's why he attended Los Angeles Trade-Technical College to study drafting. While he was in college, Campbell became part of the local club scene and developed his trademark dance moves.

The funky chicken, a southern dance, became a national hit in 1969 when Rufus Thomas recorded "Do the Funky Chicken." Campbell was having a hard time mastering the dance's rocking movement. As performed by Thomas, who even in his sixties could gyrate with the best, it was a rocking, wobbly move that involved arm movements that mimicked barnyard fowl. For whatever reason, Campbell couldn't do the dance smoothly, finding that his arms would freeze or lock, creating a comical hesitation that cracked up his friends. "No matter what type of mistake I made, they clapped," Campbell said in *The* Vibe *History of Hip Hop.*

Quickly this embarrassment became a trademark that Campbell, along with some other folks he met at LA clubs, began embellishing with leg lifts, splits, dives, and knee drops. Because people often guffawed at the locking movements, the Uncle Sam (in which he pointed at viewers à la the famous army recruiting poster) became a standard move. Another signature move, leg lifts accompanied by hands clenched together in front of the body, looked fantastic when done by two or three dancers at a time (a move echoed in Psy's "Gangnam Style" video in 2012).

After those first two nights of dancing with Campbell and company, Freeman left LA for a month to dance in a musical. Upon her return home, on a Wednesday night she went back to Maverick's Flat, where she was spotted by a *Soul Train* scout who encouraged her to audition at Denker Park that Friday. That's where she met producer Tommy Kuhn and Don Cornelius, who she recalled were dressed in smart, fly coats like the title character's in the blaxploitation flick *Shaft*. Not surprisingly, both Freeman and Campbell were invited to *Soul Train* tapings that Saturday and Sunday morning.

While Freeman and Campbell would soon be celebrated for their dancing on that very first weekend on the *Soul Train* set, the duo didn't impress Don. As soon as they went into their locking moves, several dancers complained to the staff that Freeman and Campbell were "invading" their space, as Freeman recalled. She said Don told them, "I want you two in the back over there in the corner." So they were moved behind singer Thelma Houston, away from the cameras.

Freeman, one of the few at the taping with show-business experience, wasn't very impressed with the amenities for the dancers. Lunch was a box of chicken, a Coca-Cola, and one drink of water. (I visited the *Soul Train* set in the early 1980s and will never forget seeing a mountain of Kentucky Fried Chicken boxes stacked up for the dancers.) The changing rooms were the studio restrooms. She couldn't do anything about these conditions, but she would have an impact on another backstage aspect of *Soul Train*.

Dancers were not allowed to use the studio pay phone to call parents, friends, or anyone else. Freeman wouldn't accept that and called her mother, who, upset about the restriction, called the police. The next day an LAPD officer stopped by the studio to let Cornelius know that he couldn't prevent the minors on the set from having access to a phone. They had the right to call their parents to let them know they were all right and to set up rides back home. Freeman also argued for herself and others to get *Soul Train* ID cards that would allow them to park in the studio parking lot.

The lanky lady's popularity helped *Soul Train*, but she may have created some tension with its host. "I remember Don Cornelius was looking at me angry because he didn't want the dancers to interact with guest stars," she said of her legendary dance with Joe Tex. "I just knew this would be my last time on *Soul Train*. But the episode aired, and the show's ratings went up." Whatever his reservations at the time about Damita Jo, Don would, in 1982, admit that her freestyle with Tex helped *Soul Train*'s popularity.

After she danced with Brown on the show, the Godfather invited her to open for him at a concert at the Los Angeles Memorial Sports Arena. Damita Jo brought many of the dancers she'd met at Maverick's Flat (Little Joe Chism, Scooby, Gary Keys, Alpha Omega Anderson, Perry Brown) with her, setting two precedents that would define the rest of her career: she'd quickly build a life away from *Soul Train*; and she'd empower other dancers using doors opened by her.

Freeman's first big non–*Soul Train* opportunity came via Dick Clark's *American Bandstand*, which made her a contestant in its national dance contest. Of course Freeman, dancing with *Soul Train* partner Joe Chism, won the contest and a free trip to Hawaii. In 1973 she appeared in the musical *Two Gentlemen from Verona* at the Music Center. In 1974 she danced as part of Diana Ross's show in Las Vegas. After that, her list of credits rolled on as she became a mainstay of LA show business, choreographing for TV specials and tours, including Clark's American Music Awards up through 1992. She even had a brief fling with acting, appearing in the 1980 Goldie Hawn comedy *Private Benjamin*.

Freeman's participation in *American Bandstand* was no accident. Dick Clark was very aware of the talent Don Cornelius's show was unearthing. The next year that same *American Bandstand* dance contest featured two other *Soul Train* regulars, Tyrone Proctor and Sharon Hill, and they won. But more than just poaching dancers, Clark actively tried to co-opt *Soul Train*'s black audience. (But it's a little early for that part of the story.)

After Campbell's inauspicious start on *Soul Train*, he became an influential figure via the broadcast. "For me, Don Campbell was the reason I wanted to be on that show," said Jeffrey Daniel, who was then living (and watching TV) in Grand Rapids, Michigan. "One Saturday afternoon, I saw the other dancers dancing, but this guy didn't dance. He walked down the aisle to the beat of the music, stopped, stuck out his hand, gave himself five, hunched his shoulders, and pointed. I was like, Oh my God. That just totally changed everything I knew about dance."

Daniel, who is really a scholar of popular dance's evolution, says Campbell "broke all the rules . . . when you're looking at dancing from the sixties up until that point." The twist, the monkey, and other popular dances were full-body movements with isolated movements of specific body parts, while locking "started a whole new level of body isolations from your hips to your head movements," Daniel said.

Don Campbell and the Lockers brought innovative dance moves from LA clubs to *Soul Train*.

Campbell's impact on the show was magnified by the fact that he arrived on *Soul Train* "posse deep" with his Maverick's Flat dancing buddies, including his then girlfriend Toni Basil, Adolfo "Shaba-Doo" Quinones, and Fred "Rerun" Berry, infiltrating Don's dance floor. Not only were they bringing new moves to the nation, they introduced a flamboyant style of dress that mixed a taste of 1940s zoot-suit flair with vibrant 1970s colors. "They're wearing these knickerbocker pants with the striped socks, marshmallow shoes, applejack hats that would twist on their head while they were dancing, sometimes with suspenders," Daniel recalls gleefully.

The Lockers were definitely a collection of stars. Toni

Basil, born as Antonia Christina Basilotta in Philadelphia, was already a show-business veteran when she hooked up with the Lockers. Back in 1964 she was an assistant choreographer on the legendary concert film *The T.A.M.I. Show*, which featured classic performances by James Brown, the Rolling Stones, and others. Throughout the 1960s, she made a few poorly received records while her dance career, both as a performer and choreographer, continued to prosper before she became part of the Maverick's Flat scene.

Basil would become one of the first white faces on *Soul Train*, which doesn't seem as though it was a big deal for her or the other dancers. In almost all the interviews about whether whites danced on *Soul Train*, folks don't reference her, perhaps because Basil was part of an otherwise all-black crew. Throughout the 1970s, she had a varied post–*Soul Train* career, working with dance-oriented rock groups (codirecting and choreographing two Talking Heads videos), in movies (George Lucas's *American Graffiti*), and in television (mashing up ballet's *Swan Lake* and street dance on *Saturday Night Live*). Her big pop moment came with the 1982 video-driven hit "Mickey," and she's rolled on ever since, including organizing a TV Land *Soul Train* tribute in 2005.

Fred "Rerun" Berry's light didn't shine as long as Basil's, but it was blindingly bright at its peak. On *Soul Train*, Berry stood out by having the biggest body in a crowd of skinny Californians and by developing his own unique take on locking. His move came to be known as the Slo-Mo, in which he broke down the locking moves to their essence, using his large limbs with remarkable grace. It didn't hurt that Berry had a great smile and a knack for including humor in his dance.

So Berry was well positioned in the mid-1970s when the black-cast sitcom became a TV trend. The ribald chitlin circuit comic Redd Foxx broke through with a smash NBC sitcom called *Sanford and Son* in early 1972. On the same network as *Julia*, Foxx's show, while not as raw as his legendarily raunchy stage show, was built around sexual innuendo and impeccable delivery and brought a colloquial urban attitude to American TV, the same way Al Benson had on R&B radio. Throughout the rest of the decade, black folks and laugh tracks were staples on prime-time TV with *Good Times*, *That's My Mama* (both debuting in 1974), *The Jeffersons* (1975), *What's Happening!!* (1976), *Diff'rent Strokes* (1978), and *Benson* (1979), all having their share of success.

As Fred "Rerun" Stubbs, Berry was the comic heart of *What's Happening!!*, a show that ran for three seasons on ABC. Created by Eric Monte, the black writer behind the beloved film comedy *Cooley High*, this sitcom was set in South Central LA and looked, not very deeply, at the lives of three black male teens. In every episode Berry wore a red beret and suspenders, echoes of his Lockers wardrobe, which became both his trademark and his curse. Though he was reportedly a millionaire by age twenty-nine, his "Rerun" persona and his weight made it hard for him to find acting gigs for the rest of his life.

The résumé for the rest of Berry's life was dotted with appearances built around his locking and those two red garments. An episode of the 2000s NBC series *Scrubs* was typical, with Berry in a dance sequence in his beret and suspenders and other cast members, in full comedy mode, dressed and dancing in his style. He died in 2003 of natural causes at fifty-two years old.

Despite the early prominence of the Lockers, *Soul Train* wasn't always smooth. Basil, who had more showbiz experience than her Locker peers, felt the dancers should be compensated for their contribution to the show's success. According to dance historian Naomi Bragin and *Soul Train* dancer Tyrone Proctor, Basil went to Don asking that Campbell be paid because of his popularity on the show. Not only was Basil turned down, but for a time Campbell and the Lockers were banned from the show. In fact, even locking was forbidden for a while. This conflict was short-lived, but it set a tone for the relationship between star dancers and *Soul Train*— these performers would be granted amazing exposure by the broadcast, but they'd have to make their money elsewhere. For example, aside from dancing with the Lockers, Campbell would make cash as a Chippendales dancer using the charming name King Dingaling.

Campbell and the Lockers would have a profound impact on an embryonic scene developing across the country, including in the most impoverished sections of New York City. A prime example of *Soul Train*'s impact on the emerging hip-hop scene is provided by Curtis Walker, one day to be known as rapper Kurtis Blow, who was a regular *Soul Train* viewer as a child in Harlem. "You're nine years old," said Walker, "and here comes this guy Don Campbellock [one of Campbell's nicknames, as well as the title of a 1972 single on Stanson Records] and the Campbellock Dancers, and they're dressed all wild with vibrant colors almost like clowns. They would do routines incredible to see."

Years before he'd rock microphones with hits like the gold twelve-inch "The Breaks," Walker was part of the city's break-dance scene. While the head spins and floor moves of hip-hop dancing were New York creations, the upper-body isolation moves of the Lockers were incorporated into what would become known as breakin'.

Walker: We owe a lot to those Lockers and we owe a lot to *Soul Train* . . . They actually contributed to hip-hop and the formatting of break-dance routines. The Campbellock dancers would all come out and all do a routine, and when the routine was done, they would go out and do solos. Each member would get a chance to do a solo for ten or fifteen seconds. That format served as the basis of break-dance routines all the way here in New York. It was incredible to see how the connection and the vibe was there. Those dancers set the trend for the hip-hop dancers to come.

Chapter 3

IT'S STAR TIME

||||||||||||||||||||||||||||||||||

EIGHT YEARS after riots ripped through the black neighborhoods of Los Angeles, Tom Bradley, a former policeman and city councilman, built a coalition of blacks, Hispanics, Jews, and white liberals to get elected as the city's first black mayor. Bradley, who had never been a marching, protesting street activist but rather a consummate political insider and consensus builder, would go on to be the city's longest-serving mayor in history.

But even with a black man's presence in City Hall, Los Angeles would never be a bastion of racial equality, as discriminatory real estate practices, intimidating policing, and income disparities created a very segregated metropolis. Blacks in LA who thrived did so through their own alliance building within the community. Don Cornelius would quickly build relationships with key local activists like Danny Bakewell. Bakewell, like a large percentage of black LA residents, migrated west from New Orleans and began a career in social activism in his twenties. He became president of the Brotherhood Crusade, one of the region's leading civil rights organizations, and would run it for more than thirty years. It was through Bakewell that Don met most of Los Angeles's black middle-class movers and shakers, while Don gave him access to black show business. In 1974 Bakewell founded the National Black United Fund, a national philanthropic organization that would grow to have twenty-two affiliates. Like *Soul Train*, the NBUF was very much the product of a collective desire to institutionalize the gains of the civil rights movement. Don's relationship with Bakewell would be similar to the one he'd had with Jesse Jackson in Chicago, an enduring friendship that had a strong political aspect.

Don's own political skills were in full effect as he focused on wooing the biggest names in soul music for *Soul Train*'s crucial second season. He made phone calls and had meetings and used the show itself as his most persuasive tool. Still, landing the major stars was a challenge. It took Cornelius until episode #49, in the middle of the 1972–73 season, to land James Brown, the Godfather of Soul, the biggest personality in a genre defined by outsized egos. Having Brown on the show was seen as crucial to establishing the *Soul Train* brand. Brown was also a strong believer in black capitalism, and at the time he owned a number of radio stations and should have been a natural supporter of *Soul Train*, but, according to Don, the Godfather had a difficult time grasping that the broadcast was black owned. Brown agreed to appear on the show only at the urging of his kids, who loved the dancing in season one.

Cornelius: I remember my first meeting with James Brown. He was so impressed as he looked around the studio, at the scenic studio with the set, that he asked me the same question three times. James Brown was from an era where you weren't anything big unless you had somebody, probably somebody white, backing you. Or giving you the green light, or a loan, or the funds, or who would take a piece of what you had in return for the backing. That was the era that he was from. He said, "Brother, who is backing you on this?" And I said, "Well, James, it's just, it's just me." And then he'd go to the dressing room and come back with his makeup and pass by me again, and say, "Brother, who you with on this?" I wanted to say, "You just asked me that." But out of respect I'd say, "James, it's just me." And then I guess I saw him just one more time, and he came to me and he said, "Brother, who's really behind this?" And I said, "James, it's just me."

Brown's appearance established *Soul Train*'s pedigree and made it a crucial stop not just for emerging young acts but for established stars. In that second season, major vocal groups the Isley Brothers and the O'Jays appeared on the show twice. Major Motown talents with major pop credentials such as ex-Temptations David Ruffin and Eddie Kendricks, Jermaine Jackson of the superhot teen-appeal group the Jackson Five, and Stevie Wonder, who was at the height of his creative powers, finally appeared on *Soul Train*. Aside from the O'Jays, other acts associated with the Philly sound of Kenny Gamble and Leon Huff and their publishing partner, Thom Bell, became *Soul Train* staples: Billy Paul, Harold Melvin & the Blue Notes, the Intruders, the Spinners.

Lip-synching was standard operating procedure on television. Singers came on shows and sang along to their record. That's how things were done in 1971, especially on syndicated programs like *American Bandstand*. That was Don's intention as well, and in the early days of *Soul Train* quite a few artists lip-synched because live performances were expensive and cumbersome. But ultimately Don gave in and allowed many stars to perform live, a willingness that would be a key element in separating *Soul Train* from the rest of what was on television.

Booking James Brown was a major coup for Don Cornelius, and it helped bolster *Soul Train's* early success.

Because of Don's flexibility, *Soul Train* became a prime live showcase for some of the greatest talents in black music, particularly during the 1970s. For example, a 1975 performance by Barry White and his Love Unlimited Orchestra on which the maestro did three solo hits, including "Can't Get Enough of Your Love, Babe" and several instrumentals. Neon signs behind the stage read BARRY WHITE and LOVE UNLIMITED instead of SOUL TRAIN. A Barry White–sponsored Little League baseball team, the Maestro Players, even appeared in the show.

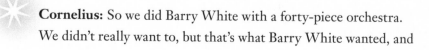

Cornelius: So we did Barry White with a forty-piece orchestra. We didn't really want to, but that's what Barry White wanted, and

Barry White was so hot at the time we were like, We're not gonna lose this booking. We gotta do what we have to do; we ended up doing Al Green with his band, and we did James Brown and the JB's, and James Brown with his whole band. We did Sly and the Family Stone, whole band. We did Tower of Power, who we hope people will remember with that, you know, superb horn section that they had. God, we did . . . and these were the most—as far as the economics were concerned, as an owner, I kind of hated it. But these were the most exciting times of my whole life. These were the most exciting experiences I had in my entire—not just my experience with the show, but in my entire life.

Don's son Tony, who would eventually spend fifteen years working on *Soul Train*, remembers the tension of the live tapings well. "The difficulty of putting together a live show as well as the excitement is you're trying to put something together mistake-free, and when you're trying to put something together mistake-free, when there's money being spent, if you can get through it, you've accomplished a whole lot. My father is thinking of the fact that people were working so hard to make sure that this live element worked. The live experience is an experience that you can't forget because you're trying to get all this done without a mistake, and with mistakes comes money lost."

White, an ex-gang member from South Central turned R&B producer-arranger turned disco love man, was one of Don's closest friends in the music industry, so it's not surprising he bit the financial bullet for him. Watching them banter during his numerous appearances throughout the seventies and early eighties was to hear a basso profundo wrestling match, wondering which man's bass voice would wrestle the other's to the ground. With White, as with so many of the soul era artists Don interviewed, you can sense the host reveling in the music and friendship.

Barry White's lush disco sound made him a *Soul Train* staple.

Al Green, who was the hottest young singer of the early seventies, introduced an updated Memphis soul sound that was spare and clean, driving on up-tempo numbers and haunting on ballads.

He appeared regularly on *Soul Train*, displaying a sexy midrange tenor and an ability to sing softly with amazing vulnerability and passion. His seven-minute performance of "Jesus Is Waiting," from his *Call Me* album, on the show in 1973 is masterful. He starts by reciting the Lord's Prayer before flowing into the gospel song with the nuance of a love song. Though people didn't turn to *Soul Train* for religious music, you can hear the crowd enjoying the testimony, especially when Green has the band bring it down low so he can sing with his trademark quiet intensity. His left arm is in a red bandanna sling, which only adds to the performance's devotional fervor.

On episode #38, Sly Stewart, of Sly & the Family Stone fame, made an equally flamboyant impression on the *Soul Train* audience. While Al Green was an ascendant star during his initial appearances, Sly was widely thought to have peaked by 1974. He was chronically late to shows, sometimes even missing them altogether. Many of the original members of his fantastic Family Stone had left the band in various disputes with its mercurial leader. But his performance of "I Want to Take You Higher," one of several of his standards performed during that taping, was a triumph of energy and musicianship.

Wearing a white hat and boots, a hot-pink, silver-sequined jumpsuit unzipped to the waist, revealing a bare chest except for a Star of David medallion, Sly plays organ, sings, and incites the crowd to sing along as he ventures among the dancers to prance and be adored. On top of all that, Sly's smile blares like the sun. The female *Soul Train* dancers giggle girlishly during a Q&A when Fawn Quinones boldly, with a lush gleam in her eye, asks if he's married. The musical chops and personal charisma that made Sly a transcendent star are incredibly evident in this performance.

Sly Stone, the front man of the influential funk and soul group Sly and the Family Stone, pictured here in all his early-seventies finery.

The sensual Marvin Gaye made his *Soul Train* debut in episode #89 in 1974. He was a notoriously reluctant performer and he especially disliked lip-synching. At that time, he was at the height of his erotic powers with his single "Let's Get It On," which had gone to No. 1 on the pop charts. During the interview he admitted, "I enjoyed doing the two numbers ["Come Get to This" and "Distant Lover"] previously—I didn't lip-synch them too well, but . . . " He then playfully answered questions from Don and the dancers before launching into "Let's Get It On," which he sang from the main floor while hugging and being hugged by various adoring women. It wasn't technically a "live" performance, since a vocal backing track is playing, but Gaye is also singing with some vigor, resulting in as interactive a performance as you'll ever see between a singer and audience. Whatever *Soul Train* rules there were about interactions between dancers and stars were wiped away by the sexual chemistry apparent that day. One of Gaye's most famous later performances on *Soul Train* had nothing to do with singing at all. Gaye, who was an avid sports fan (Detroit Lion football players Lem Barney and Mel Farr's voices had been heard on the intro to "What's Going On"), was one of Don's hangout buddies. On *Soul Train* episode #222 in 1977, Don and Gaye played a game of one-on-one with mutual friend and soul legend Smokey Robinson as referee. It was not the most gracefully played game (Gaye was winning three baskets to two when it broke for a commercial), but it was a peek into the Los Angeles black celebrity world.

Fifteen years before Arsenio Hall debuted his hip, black-oriented talk show, Cornelius's interactions with White, Gaye, Robinson, and others were a window into black glamour and privilege that was particular to Hollywood. In places like Martha's Vineyard in Massachusetts and Sag Harbor in Long Island, black folks with money had been gathering for decades to network and mate. But this was a new world, built on black music, that was also peopled by black movie and TV stars as well as behind-the-scenes players. It was a 1970s phenomenon that *Soul Train* made visible.

Marvin Gaye was both a regular presence on *Soul Train* and a close personal friend of Don Cornelius.

Another of these behind-the-scenes moments was a lovely duet between Aretha Franklin and Smokey Robinson that was recorded for a 1979 episode. The two soul legends were childhood friends from Detroit. Robinson remembers hearing her sing for the first time when she was four years old. Franklin was the daughter of Reverend C. L. Franklin, who in the 1950s was one of the most powerful religious figures in black America, while Smokey was a gifted singer-songwriter who'd eventually be signed by Berry Gordy along with his group, the Miracles. Though both were good friends from the same city, the silky-voiced songwriter and the Queen of Soul had never performed together on record or TV. Sitting together at a piano with Franklin, an outstanding gospel-trained pianist, on the keys, they sing a slow, sweet version of the Miracles' classic "Ooo Baby Baby." Franklin sings the first verse, Robinson the second, and then they sing the chorus together—not exactly harmonizing, more singing softly together in their different styles. It is a brief but magical duet that made the *Soul Train* set seem more like a living room after church on a Sunday afternoon than an LA TV studio.

As we'll see, there would be a number of *Soul Train* theme songs over the years, but one of the best was played only once on the show. Stevie Wonder, who was on during the first season, would make regular appearances over the years. His first song on a 1971 episode was "Superstition," but Wonder, on grand piano, then played a ditty called "Soul Train," with Cornelius by his side and the dancers gathered around. The hook was very simple: "*Soul Train* and Don Cornelius / Where all the brothers and sisters get together," backed by a soulful, jaunty piano riff that is similar to a melody he would use years later for "Happy Birthday."

Wonder got the dancers to sing and clap their hands in another of those intimate moments between singer and audience that made *Soul Train* feel like a window not into a TV show, but into the world of black showbiz.

Patti LaBelle, whether with Sarah Dash and Nona Hendryx in Labelle, or later as a solo artist, was a legendary live performer known for kicking off her shoes, sometimes rolling on the stage, and always singing with celestial power. Her fellow Philadelphia native Ahmir "Questlove" Thompson, leader of the Roots, doted on her *Soul Train* appearances.

Thompson: I'll say another powerful live performer of the show, who sometimes didn't perform with a band, and that was Patti LaBelle: I believe that all of her performances were sung with her actual voice. Once, Labelle had a band behind them, during the *Nightbirds* period of "Lady Marmalade" in '74, but all of her performances were powerful and very, very live. I think she's probably the only artist to garner ten-second applause at the end of the song before the animation starts. Usually a song is finished and a person does a bow, they'll clap for—they'll show the clap for one second, two seconds—and then go straight to the animation. But when she did "Somewhere Over the Rainbow," that was, I believe, December of 1981. She did "Somewhere Over the Rainbow," and it was powerful enough, even without a band, powerful enough to get, I think, the only ten-second applause before Don let the animation go.

There were scores of other remarkable live performances during the seventies on *Soul Train*. But only one pulled the covers back on the precision needed for show-business success as much as the episode in which master choreographer Cholly Atkins showed how he created the O'Jays' onstage magic. "I actually think that was Don's idea," said O'Jay member Walter Williams. "Because we used to rehearse in LA at times, and Don came by and saw how he was beating us up." The song was "Give the People What They Want," a classic Philly International message song. Viewers saw the O'Jays in street clothes and then saw them transition into the song in onstage gear. This peek behind the scenes featured show-business legend Atkins.

Atkins and legendary tap dancer Honi Coles had been a part of a team, Coles & Atkins, that was extremely popular in the 1940s and 1950s. As popular culture changed, dance teams lost favor while stand-up vocal groups, mostly composed of golden-voiced teenagers with no stage experience, came into vogue. Working out of a studio in the Ed Sullivan Theater on Broadway (where David Letterman now tapes his CBS late show), Atkins pioneered what he labeled "vocal choreography," tailoring movement to augment the doo-wop vocalizing of the day. Until Atkins's innovations, most groups just stood at the microphone and swayed a bit as they sang.

But this was the start of the rock 'n' roll era, when backbeats became louder and electric guitars and bass were introduced, shifting power in popular music to the rhythm sections. So the stagecraft had to match the music. Atkins became so popular in New York that when Berry Gordy started building his Motown Records empire in Detroit, he recruited Atkins to be part of his artist-development team. Atkins was crucial in shaping teenage groups like the Supremes and the Temptations into the most polished entertainers of the 1960s. When Motown closed its artist-development division in the 1970s, Atkins became a free agent and the O'Jays were his new professional mainstay. Eddie Levert, Walter Williams, and Sammy Strain were stellar students, so it was a treat to see Atkins help them work out the steps to the funky "Give the People What They Want."

Thompson remembered the episode vividly: "The studio's all clear and Cholly's like, Yeah, now you do one, two, three step. My mom was obsessed with Cholly Atkins. She knew who he was from Detroit, and I'm like, 'Who is that?' She's like, 'That's Cholly Atkins! He taught the Temptations how to dance. Now he's teaching the O'Jays.' Without that I wouldn't have known any of that stuff."

The intimacy between Don and the O'Jays was hard-earned and sometimes took a toll on the vocal group members' sleep. During the 1970s, when the O'Jays were a premier attraction, they'd travel to LA with no plans to do *Soul Train*. But Eddie Levert remembers that "Don would literally come to our hotel room. You'd get a call from the lobby. 'Come out, you've got to do our show.' We'd fluff him off. Finally he'd get me up, and I would say, 'Well, your boy Walter is not coming out.' He would bang on Walter's door for hours and hours. Walter would be yelling, 'Get away! Go away!' So when we got in front of the camera, all of that bantering would start. Later we would hang out, go to his house and have drinks."

It was easy to tell who Don really respected as artists, and who he had on *Soul Train* just because it was good business, by the way he introduced them and how happy he seemed to interview them. His love for the O'Jays was obvious. "I love him for how he introduced the O'Jays," the Roots' Thompson said. "His introducing the O'Jays and interviewing the O'Jays are probably his brightest moments, because besides the Jackson Five, I believe the O'Jays were the only group that he would introduce that always came with the superlative 'mighty,' as in, 'The mighty, mighty O'Jays.'" The group appeared on more than twelve episodes of the show. No act is more closely identified with *Soul Train* than this vocal trio. So when they were awarded a Lifetime Achievement Award by Black Entertainment Television (BET), Cornelius was asked to introduce them. "He told BET, 'I'm not coming out. I don't do that anymore,'" Levert said. "So they gave me his number and I told him, 'What do you mean you can't do it?'" Of course he did get there, and once again said, "The mighty, mighty O'Jays" to the delight of the singers, the live audience, and the millions watching at home.

Chapter 4

DICK CLARK'S *SOUL UNLIMITED*

||||||||||||||||||||||||||||||||||||||

IN HIS interview for VH1's *Soul Train* documentary, director Kevin Swain asked Don Cornelius about his relationship with Dick Clark and *American Bandstand*. Cornelius's reply is one of the most complex he gives during the interview, and the most interesting parts didn't end up in the final cut.

"I remember when we first got started, there were news columns that described *Soul Train* as a black *American Bandstand*," he said, "and when I first heard that term used, it kind of offended me until I thought about it. And it didn't take very long before I thought about it. It was not something to be offended by, because that's exactly what we were. We were a black *American Bandstand*. Even though in later years Dick Clark and I didn't get along real well, I would never deny that the principal inspiration for *Soul Train* was *American Bandstand* and Dick Clark. Later Dick would start his own soul dance show, but that's something we don't really talk about. It's a long story, and it might be embarrassing to one of us, and we don't talk about it."

The impact of *Soul Train* on the television landscape was not lost on Dick Clark. As mentioned, after *Soul Train*'s first season, he invited the dynamic Damita Jo Freeman and Joe Chism to compete on his national dance competition, and they won it. The next competition also featured two dancers from *Soul Train* (Tyrone Proctor and Sharon Hill), who also won. But by 1973, Clark was no longer just cherry-picking talent but actively trying to co-opt Cornelius's franchise by launching his own black-themed dance show, *Soul Unlimited*.

Launched as a special episode of *American Bandstand* on March 24, 1973, it was hosted by Buster Jones, a smooth-voiced but physically awkward Los Angeles–based announcer. Watching him interview singer Eddie Kendricks or the family vocal group Sylvers, Jones not only has no questions (Cornelius didn't always have anything to ask, either) but, unlike Cornelius, is in no way cool. He nearly trips over the microphone cord preparing to talk with the Sylvers and draws perplexed looks from Kendricks and another interviewee, Rufus Thomas. Clark should have paid someone to write Jones some questions and given the brother a capable stage manager.

Despite *Soul Unlimited*'s amateurish flavor, it still could have killed *Soul Train*. Considering Clark's power in the record and television industry, including the backing of ABC, this rip-off could have proved fatal to Cornelius's dream. But Dick Clark's power move was stopped cold.

The hero of this sad tale is Clarence Avant, one of the most powerful men in the history of the black music business and one of the most press shy. In his nearly sixty years in show business, his biggest media exposure came in the 2013 Academy Award–winning documentary *Searching for Sugar Man*, in which he's depicted as something of a villain. The film looks back at the unlikely career twists of Sixto Rodriguez, a Bob Dylan–esque singer-songwriter Avant had signed to his Sussex Records in the early 1970s, then released two critically respected albums that, between them, sold fewer than thirty thousand copies.

In a strange turn of events, Rodriguez's records found their way to South Africa, where white youth, participating in the anti-apartheid movement, made his songs, composed in Detroit in the 1970s, anthems of their 1980s movement. One part of the documentary asks what happened to Rodriguez's South African royalties. When asked, Avant replies gruffly that he knows nothing about any contracts from the 1970s.

The film's editing makes it seem as if Avant was being defensive when, in fact, Avant was just being Avant. After his almost sixty years in show business, he has acquired a blunt, tough, often obscenity-laced vocabulary that belies his skills at internal politics.

His career began back in the 1960s working for music-booking powerhouse Joe Glaser, who famously managed Louis Armstrong but also ran a booking agency that once handled the touring activities of more than a thousand artists. Avant was one of the first blacks to be part of Glaser's team and built a network of connections within the white, largely Jewish world of touring and management that would be the backbone of his career. His personal management of composer Lalo Schifrin would be crucial during the 1960s and early 1970s because the Argentinean's jazz-influenced style would make him Hollywood's hottest composer, knocking out gritty film scores (*Dirty Harry*, *Bullitt*) and beloved TV themes (*The Man from U.N.C.L.E*, *Mission: Impossible*). The contacts Avant made working for Glaser and the visibility of Schifrin's work gave Avant unusual access to the halls of power.

After moving from New York to Los Angeles in the late 1960s, he set up Venture Records, a joint venture between MGM Records and former Motown A&R director William "Mickey" Stevenson. The company became the blueprint for collaborations between major labels and black entrepreneurs to come. A few years later, Avant would start his own label, Sussex, which would enjoy massive pop hits by Bill Withers ("Lean on Me," "Ain't No Sunshine"), some minor hits

(Creative Source's "Who Is He and What Is He to You"), and the now internationally revered flops of Rodriguez.

"My relationship with Clarence started almost the day I hit Los Angeles to start doing *Soul Train*," Don recalled. "He was so enthusiastic for what we were doing that he started calling people at networks, saying, 'This *Soul Train* show should be on a network.'" Sitting in his Wilshire Boulevard office in 2012, Avant, in typically brusque fashion, says, "There were only three networks then. I knew someone at all three, and they all said no."

By 1973 Avant was a consultant to ABC, so when Dick Clark was planning *Soul Unlimited*, he invited the black executive in for a sit-down. "I knew Dick Clark a little bit," Avant recalled. "One of the ABC execs set up the meeting. Dick Clark wanted my okay. He wanted me to endorse his idea. I freaked out. 'If you do this, there's no Don Cornelius,' I told him. We had just gotten free enough to have something on TV. I told Dick Clark no—I would not endorse his show."

Outraged by Clark's power move, black political leaders, led by Chicago's Reverend Jesse Jackson, contacted Clark and ABC executives to protest. Many in the black community felt that having a black-owned show on television wasn't just cool TV, but an extension of the civil rights movement. The idea that Clark, with whom blacks had always had an uneasy relationship, could kill *Soul Train* led to threats of an ABC boycott.

Avant set up a meeting with top ABC executives in New York—even though he'd already received a threatening letter from William Morris, which was representing Dick Clark Productions. "It was a short letter telling me to stay out of their business," he said. Avant met with ABC chairman (and founder) Leonard Goldenson and president Eldon H. Rule. Avant didn't hold back: "I was very upset, very upset. If Dick Clark had been allowed to do it, then there would have been no Don Cornelius."

And when the meeting was over, so was *Soul Unlimited*.

Don Cornelius never spoke with Dick Clark before his death, and Clarence Avant didn't speak to Clark again for some twenty years. Not only did this end the threat to *Soul Train*, but it perhaps influenced ABC's management to open its doors to more black content. In the 1970s ABC would produce several black sitcoms, make *Soul Train* announcer Sid McCoy the first black staff announcer on its radio and TV network, and, in 1977, green-light the historic slavery miniseries *Roots*.

Avant continued to be a busy behind-the-scenes force in the black music business in the early 1970s. In 1971 he was one of those who started KAGB, LA's first African American–controlled radio station. Two years later, he persuaded the Ford Foundation to finance a music documentary, *Save the Children*, about a massive concert/political event organized by Reverend Jesse Jackson's Operation PUSH in Chicago. But his role in the *Soul Train* saga is far from over. Avant, one of Don's closest friends and business advisors, will be heard from again.

DANCER PROFILE: Tyrone Proctor

The gay contribution to black popular culture is usually ghettoized to books about gay culture. But it would be impossible to disconnect any discussion of *Soul Train* dance from gay club culture. A number of the dancers on the show were gay, and it was never a big deal. Don and his staff accepted it as a given. They recruited the best dancers they could find, and showcased them to a national audience. Dancer Jody Watley remembers: "Though unspoken, *Soul Train* had an obvious black male gay culture going on, and for that reason the show was also quite forward. Don allowed everyone to be themselves on camera—that's clear when you watch old clips."

So black gay culture, while diluted, was given a platform on *Soul Train* in ways big and small—but probably the most overt example was a dance called waacking. Like many early-1970s dances, waacking isolated body parts (in this case largely the arms and hands), using them to move through space like summer fans in church ladies' hands with great speed and an exaggerated femininity, elbows bent and arms twirling. Via *Soul Train*, an expression of gay subculture went mainstream.

The primary exponent of waacking on the show was Tyrone Proctor, also known as the Bone, who lived with his family in Philadelphia and dreamed of being a dancer on *Soul Train*. Against the wishes of his father, the teenager saved up his cash and trekked out to the West Coast. The lanky, large-Afroed young man didn't know anybody in the City of Angels and was desperately seeking a way into the dance scene when he saw a poster on a light pole promoting a party. Proctor walked into the party and his life changed. There were Don Campbell and

Patti Davis and Rerun and many of the *Soul Train* dance stars. Proctor felt the floor shaking under the power of the dancers inside.

Proctor quickly befriended Little Joe Chism, a charismatic mover who'd become a viewer favorite during those early *Soul Train* seasons.

Proctor: Joe would take me to different places because he wanted me to see LA. He was the glue who kept everybody together. He was the one who got me on *Soul Train*. He knew a lot about things good, bad, and indifferent. He kept everyone informed and together. No one disliked Joe.

One of the places he took me was a gay club called the Paradise Ballroom. I'll never forget it. They played the Temptations' "Papa Was a Rolling Stone." It was so funny. The beat was like boom, boom, boom, boom. People were posing to the whole beat. They had a pole in the middle of the floor. They were on top of the pole in the ceiling posing. All on the beat. It was phenomenal. I think Don did that on *Soul Train* one time because there's footage of that. When he did it on *Soul Train*, it was a rather poor version of what you saw in the clubs, but nevertheless, it was done. I'm sure Don was aware there were many gay dancers on *Soul Train*, but he turned a blind eye.

There's a gentleman who danced on the show called Lamont Peterson, who was a formidable, formidable dancer. I mean, there were many dancers on there that are formidable, but Lamont was really good with the posing. And I believe through that evolved what you know now as waacking, because there was Lamont doing it.

People always come up to me and ask me how did the name *waack* come. The name *waack* came because I was showing someone to do it, and I kept telling them, "You gotta whack your arm," and that's where the name comes in. The two a's came in because we didn't want to get it confused with the word *wack*, which had a negative connotation. So we said, we'll put another *a* in there, and we'll change the whole thing. That's how we did that.

Daniel: There were other people before Tyrone who were the premier waack dancers, who came up with a lot of basics to the steps. But Tyrone—I would have to say I credit him with bringing that dance to *Soul Train*. It didn't have a name yet. They called it "punking" at first for the fact that that dance came out of gay clubs. It was just before discos really boomed and started opening. And Tyrone took me to a club so I could see this dance. He said, "Jeffrey, you've got to come to this club, the Paradise Ballroom. You've got to see this dance." The reason why the dance has the name *waacking* was because of the way Tyrone was teaching it to us. He said, "You got to whack your arm. You got to whack your head. You got to whack to the music." Up to today he's the premier waack dancer, so if you gotta know waacking, come to the waack doctor, Tyrone Proctor.

Proctor: At the straight clubs then, the DJ would be on the mic promoting some event or himself and they'd be playing a whole lot of soul music. At the gay club, they were concerned about the sound system, and they'd be playing straight-up disco and the focus would be on dancing. So we began attracting straights. A lot of people don't know that the bump came out of those gay clubs and then moved into the mainstream. Waacking wasn't the only dance of that era to move out from the gay clubs. I got a special appreciation for waacking 'cause I learned it from the best.

Waacking has become part of the international dance catalog. Proctor still teaches the moves at workshops from Russia to Hong Kong, from Shanghai to Argentina, where he can attract up to a thousand anxious students. But he is far from alone. For example, a look on the website of Steps NYC, one of Manhattan's top locations for amateurs to learn and professionals to rehearse, shows a waacking class being offered. A video of an instructor in Finland, a young white woman, teaching this once-underground gay dance to a class of awkward wannabe dancers is quite entertaining. This journey of an expression—music, dance, language—from underground to the globe was a route that so much African American culture took in the twentieth century. That waacking was an overtly gay expression (as opposed to covert) adds another layer to the tale.

Waacking, which definitely shares kinship with Don Campbellock's playful locking and anticipates the voguing of New York gay culture in the early 1990s, would be a major inspiration for many nongay dancers who'd find celebrity on *Soul Train*, especially the gifted Daniel.

Though born in LA, Jeffrey Daniel's family moved to Grand Rapids, Michigan, when he was a kid, where he suffered sunshine envy.

Daniel: I'm watching *Soul Train* every Saturday thinking and thinking, Why am I in Grand Rapids? I need to go back to LA. I was still in high school. And I met Tyrone at Maverick's Flat. One day I'm in there dancing, and I look over and I see Tyrone. I'm like, "Oh my God, it's Tyrone the Bone." I used to see him in *Right On!* magazines and watch him on TV every week. So Tyrone was doing the steps. I knew all his steps from watching him on TV, so I'm doing the steps with him. So anyway, we start dancing together, and from that we became friends. I went back to Grand Rapids, and I was going to school, and I finally came back to LA and I went to Tyrone's place and he took me to *Soul Train* with him. He said, "Okay, Jeffrey, I'm gonna get you in." He got me in, but they said,

"He can come in, but he can't dance. You can just sit down." So I went there, and I sat down.

Daniel was lucky enough to begin his *Soul Train* experience with the taping of memorable episodes #141 and #142. "Barry White was up there with his full orchestra," he remembers. "Elton John came up there with a glass piano. I'm sitting there watching this, and the music came on. I got up and I danced anyway. And the guy came over and said, 'Yeah, I saw you dance anyway. I saw you out there.' He embarrassed me in front of everyone. You know what you can do. I credit Tyrone for helping me get onto *Soul Train* and helping me kick-start my whole career and everything."

Thanks to Proctor, waacking went from the gay club culture into the mainstream of the show. The Outrageous Waack Dancers, as Proctor and his crew were known, became one of the show's core dance groups: "It was the Lockers, Something Special, who were another small dance crew, the Waackers, and the Electric Boogaloos. Now, not everyone who was on *Soul Train* during that era was a great dancer. A lot folks were poseurs. Someone who couldn't really dance but just looked good. You could just dress beautifully and be stylish. Or you could dance really well." Proctor is a little too modest to say that with his round Afro, wide smile, and dancing skills he embodied all three types. It was as a student of movement that he inspired Daniel's dancing.

Daniel: Tyrone taught me how to listen inside the music. I've always sang. I've always been around music, but he taught me. He would be dancing to a song, and there would just be one string line, it would just go *zip*, and all of a sudden Tyrone would just move with it. And I was like, "Tyrone, how did you know that's there?"

He said, "Jeffrey, you got to listen to the music." I attribute that to me becoming a choreographer and a producer, because he really taught me how to listen in the music and hear every instrument, every sound. You can dance to anything. Like you can dance to the voice. Tyrone will be dancing to the music, and all of a sudden he'll just pantomime the vocal of the song.

The combo of Proctor and Daniel not only became star dancers on the show but, like precocious children, had the run of the place backstage too. "It would be fair to say that Tyrone Proctor and myself—we're kind of like Don Cornelius's prodigal sons," says Daniel. "I mean, we would get away with things that just no other dancer could even dream of."

"When you go downstairs, that's where the hubbub is," Proctor recalled. "That's where the producers are, that's where the hairdressers are, that's where the greenroom is, and no dancers were ever allowed to go down there. So Jeffrey and I would go down there. At that time I had a lot of hair, and I would go down there and get my hair done, trying to be a star or something. Then Jeffrey could go down there. We were the only two that could go and talk to guests. Don Cornelius, I think, favored us. We could get away with a lot of stuff. One of the things I noticed as the show went on, Don kept adding black crew. At first there were only white faces behind the camera, but each season we got more dark faces. Don got a lot of people in the industry in LA through the show."

"Don stood by the monitors while he was watching the action on *Soul Train*," Daniel said. "Dancers just didn't go over to Don. But for Tyrone and me, it wasn't off-limits. We could go over there and speak to Don. We just didn't abuse our privileges. Don actually gave us money. I really want to say this, because people think Don is just this hard shell of a person, which he is, but Don is a sweet person. Tyrone got arrested for traffic violations. He wasn't a criminal. Just traffic violations. And we're at a taping. Where's Tyrone? Don sent me and [production coordinator] Chuck Johnson down there with the money, and we got Tyrone out of jail, and Don Cornelius paid to get him out so he can come and dance on the show."

It isn't surprising that Proctor ended up with traffic tickets, since he and his fellow waackers were notorious for what they called the Chinese fire drill. "At a red light, we would put the car in park, and we would jump out and just dance all around the car, and then when the light would change, we would jump back in the car and take off again," said Daniel, adding, "The people would be mad behind us. They would be upset, but we would be in there living our lives. It would be so funny. So, so, so funny."

Proctor would be recruited to dance on *American Bandstand*. When Damita Jo Freeman and Joe Chism won Dick Clark's national dance championship, they recommended Sharon Hill and Proctor for the next contest.

Proctor: There was, I think, about seven or eight contestants. We were the only black couple in the contest, and out of the hundred thousand votes tabulated, Sharon and I got sixty thousand of the votes. That's what was told to us. It was unbelievable. I remember to this day winning the car, and what I did. I just jumped up and just fell on the car. It was a Mazda RX-4 coupe. They called me, and they said, "There's only one glitch." I said, "What's that?" They said, "You need $334.28 in order to pick the car up," and I'm like, "Well, why do I need that?" And he said, "That's the taxes you gotta pay." And I'm going, "Oh, God, where am I gonna get this money at?"

Frustrated by this turn of events, Proctor reached out to the only person he knew who might have the cash to help him pay the taxes—Don Cornelius. Because of the bad blood between *Soul Train* and *American Bandstand*, Don could have easily said no, viewing Proctor's participation in Dick Clark's contest as a betrayal. But Don looked beyond that history to help a young friend in need. "So we went up to Don Cornelius very humbly and he just sat there and wrote the check out. We went downstairs, cashed it, and I got my car. Sharon got a car as well."

Having danced on both *Soul Train* and *American Bandstand* during the height of their 1970s rivalry, Proctor has some interesting observations about the experience.

Proctor: Very different. Very different but very similar. Everybody was copying what we were doing. Everybody. James Brown always stood his own, and I respect a man for that. I never try to do anything he might have tried to do—a robot maybe one or two times, but other than that, no. But you know that's how popular [*Soul Train*] was. It was no different from *Bandstand*, because they were trying to vie for the same group of fans that we had. You have to also understand that these two shows are taped in the same city. So there's gonna be similarities. The only difference is the skin color. On *Bandstand*, you saw a lot more Caucasians and Mexican Americans than you did on *Soul Train*. On *Soul Train* there were more African Americans. We had other nationalities on there, but it wasn't as prevalent as the African Americans that were on there.

[Going to *Bandstand*], I felt nervous at first. You feel like a little turncoat because you're on a whole different show. But Dick Clark and his crew were extremely nice. The kids on the show were very accepting. We got on the show, and again it wasn't—it didn't have anything to do with color. We were just so happy to be on there just dancing.

One of the most identifiable *Soul Train* dancers didn't introduce any landmark moves. She was simply the most notable nonblack regular in the show's long history. Her name is Cheryl Song—also known as the Asian girl with the long hair.

Song lived in the middle of a contradiction. Her mother and father ran a very traditional, strict Asian household in the middle of overwhelmingly black South Central. She attended Dorsey, one of the city's top black high schools. So when Song's parents told her, "Don't hang around with black people," something had to give. Song said, "I had a pretty tumultuous childhood growing up, and I felt like I didn't fit in anywhere. The only thing I knew is that I liked to dance. I guess that was my release.

"So when I was in high school, one of the dancers, I guess his name was Dane, brought me on *Soul Train* as a dare, because, you know, I wasn't black. He brought me on, and they liked me. So I was able to stay on the show, and it was the happiest time of my life. It was because it was somewhere where I finally meant something to people, and they would recognize me, and I was like, 'Wow, somebody knows me!' So it was kind of like my little clique that I could belong to. And if I didn't have *Soul Train* as something to look forward to, I just don't know how my life would have ended up."

Song's parents were not so enthused. "They said, 'What are we going to tell our relatives?' I was just like, 'Just don't tell them!' . . . We were taught to save face, which meant whatever was going on in your life personally, you always had to give the impression that things were well. That's just the way it was. Because my parents were so rigid, I didn't know what it was like to be hugged or told 'I love you,' and I finally felt like someone liked me when I was on *Soul Train*, so that's why it meant so much to me."

Cheryl Song's long hair made her famous among *Soul Train* viewers.

Song's warm recollection shouldn't disguise the fact that the reception was not that warm when she first arrived on Cornelius's set. Like a lot of people who look back on *Soul Train*, there is the tendency to initially see things through rose-colored glasses, but, with a little prodding, a more complex experience emerges.

Song: Well, the first time I went on, I remember everyone kind of stopped and said, Oh, look! Because there's this Asian girl, and it's like, Where did she come from? So I remember that I got to dance a few times, and they ended up liking me, the staff, so they kept me on, and I thought everything was just so beautiful. And, "Wow! I can't believe I'm actually here." I remember one time they put me on the riser, and I was standing there in the center of the riser and somebody said, "Who's that high yellow bitch think she is?" Then I was scared. Oh my God, I'm gonna get jumped! I was really, really scared. I remember as soon as the show was over, I, like, ran to my car so that I wouldn't get jumped or assaulted or something like that. Then I realized, Wow. Certain people hate me. So it always puzzled me that people could just have feelings like that towards me.

Song became something of a flash point on the show. There were definitely haters of the long-haired Asian dancer among the other dancers and some of the viewers, but overall Song was accepted, an acceptance that meant she was subject to the same challenges every *Soul Train* dancer faced—getting close to the camera. "It was pretty competitive. I remember we would all be dancing as soon as the music played, but the minute that camera came towards you, and you saw that red light, someone would jump in front of you. Then you would go back and try to jump in front of them. That was a little frustrating, but, hey, you had to do what you had to do to get on camera."

Over time, her *Soul Train* celebrity somewhat softened her family's attitude toward her.

> **Song:** Probably some people must have said to them, "Oh, your daughter's on *Soul Train*," and finally, maybe they got the idea that that's a good thing instead of something to be ashamed of. So they kind of accepted it. It was just bashed into my head, no matter what you do, you're going to major in mathematics or chemistry or science. And me being so young, I thought, Well, if I do what they want me to do, I'll end up just as unhappy as they are. So when they told me that that's what I was going to be majoring in in college, it's gonna be math or science, I said, No, no, it's not. And I was a dance major in college.

One of Song's most unlikely reflections on her *Soul Train* years is that no dancers on the show ever asked her out, and no one ever asked her to dance when she went out. "Nobody did! Nobody!" she said. As hard as it is to imagine that the most famous Asian woman in black TV history was ignored by men, that's Song's story and she's sticking to it. "Probably because I was Asian, but I remember going to clubs in Los Angeles, and they were mostly black, but that's who I felt comfortable with. So I would end up sitting there the whole night all by myself. And so I was like, nobody ever asked me to dance. I don't know if they were afraid, or I don't know, but most of the times I would just end up sitting there. So I remember one day, Howard Hewitt, he was in Shalamar. He asked me to dance because he felt sorry for me. But that was like one of the few times I got to dance when I went out."

Gap Band lead singer (and notorious ladies' man) Charlie Wilson has put it on record that he tried to "holler at" Song, as have some other entertainers who performed on *Soul Train*, but apparently she was oblivious.

Whether Song was asked out or not, it's clear that entertainers and their management were very aware of her. She helped the Commodores choreograph one of their tours and was cast in numerous 1980s videos, including Rick James's "Super Freak" and Michael Jackson's "Beat It."

Watch closely and you can spot her in the opening diner sequence of that landmark video.

Tyrone Proctor, bringing gay culture to the masses, and Cheryl Song, a nonblack face in a sea of Afros, were each in their own way iconic figures on *Soul Train*. Waacking-influenced moves are still employed by choreographers and found in twenty-first-century music videos from Lady Gaga, among others, while gifted Asian street dancers are now staples of our culture, from Gap commercials to competition shows like *America's Best Dance Crew*. Though decades removed from their *Soul Train* appearances, the legacy of Proctor and Song flows on.

Chapter 5

TSOP

||||||||||||||||||||||||||||||||||||||

THE SECOND—AND greatest—*Soul Train* theme song resulted from a brief collaboration between Don Cornelius and the premier R&B writing-producing team of Kenny Gamble and Leon Huff. This pair began as independent producers in the 1960s, when they created hit singles for Jerry Butler, Wilson Pickett, and Joe Simon, among many. This catapulted the Philadelphia-based duo to the mantle of R&B's top creative force. In 1971 Gamble and Huff made a deal with CBS Records to found Philadelphia International Records as a vehicle for funneling all their energy into acts on their own label.

Together, and in collaboration with several exceptional staff writers (John Whitehead, Gene McFadden, Bunny Sigler, Cynthia Biggs, Dexter Wansel), PIR was a powerhouse that developed stars (the O'Jays, Harold Melvin & the Blue Notes, Teddy Pendergrass) and enduring songs ("Wake Up Everybody," "Love Train," "For the Love of Money," "Me and Mrs. Jones," "Love Is the Message," "Ain't No Stoppin' Us Now") using a lush, intricate, rhythmically intense sound built around gospel-inspired singing and the talents of a remarkable team of session musicians.

Labeled MFSB (Mother Father Sister Brother), these players, anchored by guitarist Norman Harris, bassist Ronnie Baker, and drummer Earl Young, worked primarily out of the City of Brotherly Love's Sigma Sound. Factoring in the more ballad-oriented songs of producer Thom Bell for the Spinners and the Stylistics, the music coming out of Philadelphia became as essential to the 1970s as the *Godfather* movies and the Watergate break-in.

When Don ran into Gamble in New York in 1973, both men were on the cusp of big things. Don wanted a new theme, one that was unique to the show and more contemporary than the funky jazz song he'd been using. So he traveled to Philadelphia and sat down with Gamble, Huff, and arranger Bobby Martin. A basic rhythm track was developed with a strutting rhythm, later augmented by a cool horn-and-string arrangement that was smooth enough for dancing, yet had a memorable melody.

Don loved the track and asked that his show's title be included in the primarily instrumental track. The female vocal group the Three Degrees sang "Soul Train, Soul Train" over four notes. The record branded the show and reflected a sound that would soon be labeled disco. He wanted the song held off any recordings until *Soul Train*'s next season. But as Gamble and Huff played the track for CBS executives and other PIR staffers, it became clear this *Soul Train* theme could be more than the opening of a TV show. So Gamble called Cornelius and said he wanted to use the song as a single off an MFSB album.

This is where Don made a strategic mistake. Instead of going along with the idea as a tool to further expose the show, he felt that the release of it as a single would infringe on his copyright and wasn't in the spirit of the agreement he'd made with PIR. So he asked Gamble and Huff to remove his show's title from the single version. The reworked song had the Three Degrees singing "People all over the world" as a hook and had a second vocal section that was simply "Let's get it on / It's time to get down." Otherwise it was the same track Cornelius would use on *Soul Train*.

Released in the spring of 1974, the song, now titled "TSOP (The Sound of Philadelphia)," went to No. 1 on both the pop and R&B charts. Instead of being a commercial for *Soul Train* that announced the show's name all over America, it worked to brand Philadelphia's new musical movement. While there's no question the original version was great for the show, Don's decision cost him a marketing opportunity for the ages.

It wasn't the last time Don wouldn't fully benefit from one of his great recording ideas.

Chapter 6

RIGHT ON

||||||||||||||||||||||||||||||||||

ONE OF the unintended consequences of the civil rights movement would be, starting in the 1970s, the targeting of black teenagers as a consumer market. White teens were already a significant cultural and consumer force through the rise of rock 'n' roll in the 1950s, with AM Top 40 radio and *American Bandstand* as direct beneficiaries. Soft drinks and acne-relief creams like Clearasil filled the coffers of radio stations and the ABC network for decades as each generation moved in and out of that angst-ridden demographic. The white teen idols Clark promoted and, in some cases, controlled also fed an appetite for fanzines like *Tiger Beat*, which titillated teens with public-relations-created tales of pinup boys and girls.

Black students of the 1960s were identified with sit-ins and protest, with noble struggle and the raised fists. But this visibility also alerted many to the massive buying these ambitious young people represented. Once they could legally sit at lunch counters, black teens became a hot new consumer market. And *Soul Train* emerged as the perfect venue to exploit this new reality. *Soul Train* was deeply intertwined with various kinds of marketers, whether advertising agencies or pulp-magazine publishers seizing the new opportunity. UniWorld and Burrell Advertising and *Right On!* magazine had very different relationships to *Soul Train*, yet all spoke to ways in which the show expanded the impact of black consumers in general and black youths in particular.

As noted earlier, 1971 was a benchmark year in black entrepreneurship, with *Soul Train*'s move to LA proving to be one of the most visible events. In that same year, Thomas Burrell and his partner Emmett McBain opened Burrell McBain advertising in Chicago. Burrell, who is now viewed as something of the patron saint of black advertising, was born in Chicago and took a high school aptitude test that suggested he had the right temperament for influencing people.

In 1961, right out of college, he got a job in the mail room of a local ad agency. Within two years, he was writing ad copy. For the rest of the 1960s, Burrell moved in search of opportunity, working for an agency in London for two years, then moving to New York before heading back to Chicago to form his own agency. His guiding philosophy was "Black people are not dark-skinned white people," meaning that you can't just use the same techniques to reach black consumers as white. Burrell would sell this difference to clients and build an enduring business.

One of Burrell McBain's first clients was Johnson Products. George Johnson gave Burrell's new company a shot, and it would be this agency that created so many of the beloved Afro Sheen commercials that are as much a part of the 1970s *Soul Train* as Don's voice. Between 1971 and 1974 Burrell would win accounts from McDonald's and Coca-Cola, accounts that would then turn into ad buys and commercials on *Soul Train*. In 1974 McBain left the company, but the renamed Burrell Advertising has continued to roll with mainstream clients to this day. Michelle Garner, a former Burrell executive, said, "These were marketers who had become savvy, and they knew the importance of the African American market, and so they initiated efforts, similar to the music business, where they had black divisions to help market to that particular consumer segment."

Soul Train was both a catalyst and beneficiary of this new respect for black consumers. It's certainly an idea Byron Lewis, founder of the UniWorld Group in 1969, agrees with.

"It changed my advertising landscape," Lewis said of the show. "It's very difficult for ethnic agencies, particularly African American advertising agencies, because we just don't have the critical mass; we are basically working on a niche and the idea of credibility, the ability to attract talent, the ability to grow, was really enhanced by *Soul Train*, because as much as we depended upon black magazines and newspapers . . . the television media reached the most people, and *Soul Train* gave us an exciting venue to place our commercials and to, frankly, get clients to give us more work to do, which really enhanced our growth."

With *Soul Train* as a platform, UniWorld was able to place ads on the show from AT&T, Eastman Kodak, Burger King, Pepsi-Cola, and Colgate. But getting those ad buys approved wasn't always easy. Lewis recalled that most of these clients initially balked at buying time on *Soul Train* "because it was difficult for them to conceive of a need to talk to African American consumers on a direct basis. But as the show became more popular, the advertisers were anxious to be on *Soul Train* . . . Anything you do well in the African American community broadens the reach into the general community, so that the advertisers always felt that doing a very good job in the black community paid double benefits."

As an architect of commercials that appeared on the show, Lewis strongly believes that they were crucial in reshaping the image of blacks in the American mind.

Lewis: Positive views of black life and experience were almost never seen in the mass media. A great deal of harm had been done to people of color, and the advertising industry had to be forced to bring people into the communication industry . . . The idea of the visual representation of blacks in a positive way was very necessary to move forward in this country. I was bred within the print medium; television was a far more effective medium to present us in a bigger and better way. I think that can also be attributed to Don, to *Soul Train*, because that's all there was.

When model Beverly Johnson appeared in an Afro Sheen commercial, she was a beneficiary of this new world of black TV advertising.

Johnson: That's where as a model you made money in advertising. So being in an Afro Sheen ad was a big payday and made me popular in the community. It was a product that actually addressed the Afro, to make sure our Afros were shining and gleaming and beautiful. It was really important that Madison Avenue finally got that they had to start doing marketing particularly for the African American community. And that's why that product was the all-time most successful African American beauty product ever.

The Roots' Ahmir Thompson, a longtime user of Afro Sheen, says his favorite of the product's ads featured abolitionist leader Frederick Douglass. "This young student is imagining he's having a conversation with Frederick Douglass," he said. "And the ghost of Frederick Douglass is sort of looking at him with that stern look. Basically he tells the student his 'fro is not tight, and that if he used Afro Sheen, he'd be tighter. So, of course, the guy applies it to his hair, it does a fade-out, and comes back with his quall perfect. And then Frederick Douglass, *poof*, disappears. Education and entertainment and business savvy in one fell swoop."

In September 1965, the Laufer brothers, Chuck and Ira, founded a teen-appeal magazine called *Tiger Beat*. Its first issue featured the white soul singers the Righteous Brothers, British invasion band Herman's Hermits, and TV music show host Lloyd Thaxton, along with a laundry list of mid-sixties pop stars, some we remember (the Beatles, the Beach Boys) and many we don't (Freddy and the Dreamers, Derek Taylor, Jan and Dean). There is a strong Anglophile bias to the names on the list, with young British bands then the hottest craze in pop.

Six years later, in 1971—that busy year of black media expansion—the owners of *Tiger Beat* started a new magazine they titled *Right On!*, the two words being the official phrase of affirmation for early-1970s black youth. The big reason *Right On!* was created was the Jackson Five, who had begun their career with four No. 1 singles. There had never been a run like that by a teen-appeal black group. Moreover, here were five handsome, big-Afroed boys, beautifully styled by Motown, to appeal to young women and be admired by young men. In the 1960s, Motown had called itself the Sound of Young America. With the Jackson Five, the label was providing the look of young America as well.

Although a few groups, white and black, tried to imitate the Jackson Five's youthful appeal (the Osmond Brothers, the Five Stairsteps, the Sylvers), the dancers of *Soul Train* were the next-biggest beneficiary of *Right On!*'s existence. "The reason we featured so many of the dancers in the magazine was because fan magazines are always using mail as a barometer as to what they should cover," said Cynthia Horner, a Californian who joined the magazine working in the mail room and quickly rose to be its editor. "The *Soul Train* dancers started getting fan letters."

Lloyd Boston, the twenty-first-century style guru with four best-selling books to his credit and innumerable TV appearances, was a regular purchaser of *Right On!* while he was growing up in New Jersey. "It wasn't beautifully produced, but you didn't know that when you were eleven or twelve," he recalled. "All you know is you saw big full-page photos of your heartthrobs, and you saw the celebrities that you knew and loved in pull-out posters in the middle . . . You would learn more about the people you watched on mute, basically, because they never really spoke. They just moved and expressed themselves with their moves and their clothes. [*Right On!*] was almost like our own little portable *Soul Train*."

To emphasize this connection between the show and the magazine, dancers would often be hired to write for *Right On!* For a time in the 1970s, popular dancer Little Joe Chism wrote a column called "And That's the Tea," "tea" being LA slang at the time for gossip, which mostly related happenings at Hollywood parties.

Horner developed an up-close and personal relationship with the dancers that would continue for several decades. "We would hang out a lot in Hollywood," Horner said. "Go to the beach sometimes. The parks. I just wanted to find out more about them because I was so fascinated with all these people that had such good heads on their shoulders and had such a sense of style. Back in those days, we didn't have fashion stylists or wardrobe coordinators. So these dancers would just figure out on their own what looked good on them, what would attract the most attention on camera."

Right On! was there from the beginning with *Soul Train* and would play a crucial role in the elevation of several later *Soul Train* dancers from TV stars to recording stars. But Horner's comments lead us to look at the third pillar of *Soul Train*'s early appeal.

Chapter 7
STYLIN'

|||||||||||||||||||||||||||||||||

OVER THE years, whenever *Soul Train* is used as a pop culture reference—be it in *I'm Gonna Git You Sucka* in 1988 or *The Fresh Prince of Bel-Air* in 1994 or the *Charlie's Angels* movie in 2000—it always evokes a time of platform shoes, applejack caps, and bell-bottoms, as if the show exists as a style time capsule of 1970s funkiness. The holy trinity of *Soul Train*'s appeal was music, dance, and fashion: both the Soul Train Gang and the performing guest artist let loose with freaky, fantastic threads that have been much imitated, parodied, but never quite duplicated.

One of the future fashion figures influenced by *Soul Train* was a white kid from Corpus Christi, Texas, named Todd Oldham, who became a force in American fashion after being named top new fashion talent by the Council of Fashion Designers in 1991. Oldham's playful vision, both in design and on camera, have made him a staple of American runways and national TV. His work as former creative director for Old Navy, his line for Target, and his role as a host for shows on MTV and Bravo speak to Oldham's mass appeal.

Labelle's flamboyant dress was matched by the intensity of their *Soul Train* performances.

He recalled growing up in Texas in the 1960s and 1970s "when the color lines were not quite as blurry as they are now," but that "thankfully, for that great moment that *Soul Train* was on, everything was cool. I can't tell you how many line dances my sister and I did down the living room with the TV."

As a child, Oldham was developing his own sense of what constituted good fashion sense, and *Soul Train* helped define it for him.

Oldham: Loads and loads of high-waisted pants were sort of the moment for *Soul Train*, a very long moment actually. Whether you were a guy or a girl, it just worked. You could do anything in them. I think the manufacturer was called Angel Flight, and their trick was that they cut pants without side seams. The seams went up the front and kind of arched on the back for extra movement. But you had to wear it with your great little puffy shirt and your short elastic things. All through the seventies, those super-high-waisted pants really worked. I know *Soul Train* helped magnify it, but I think it was a style that had been resonating for a while. Up until about the mid-1970s is when we lost this mass cooperation with our public psyche. At that point seventy-year-old insurance men were wearing pants the same as a young kid. We don't get that cooperation anymore. So you had everybody tweaking and interpreting one silhouette.

Bright colors were a huge part of the 1970s *Soul Train* fashion palette, which was happening in mainstream design but "really kind of reflects what was going on in ethnic fashion," Oldham believes.

Oldham: It started making acceptable things like tighter clothes on men and some of those colors. I mean the colors are kind of freaky. It's hard to talk people into wearing lime pantsuits now. It was a lot easier at that time, apparently. There was always a kind of simple classic form with the clothes on *Soul Train*, but there was always a kind of unusual detail, like some of the embroideries. Always had some sort of 'I visited Morocco' thing going on. And then there were the colors. Everything was so seriously turned up. Like weird, off colors. Like a giant pancreas on the stage. I don't know if it was propriety or what exactly made people's decisions, but it was a much more free approach. It was daring, but they didn't seem to be as concerned at trying to be acceptable.

Classic seventies fashion and hair.

A feature that really caught the embryonic designer was that many couples on the show wore the same outfits. Oldham says, "People were there together. That's what made it work. It kind of magnified the moves when your outfits are the same, and it wasn't exactly androgynous dressing, even though they're the same clothes."

Oldham's eye for style made him fascinated by Don Cornelius's choices. His thoughts are not always flattering, but they are amusing.

Oldham: His clothes kind of looked like drawings of clothes, because they were polyester at the time, and they almost looked like flat cutouts if you look closely—because they were kind of poured clothes. So he has a strange presence . . . Don Cornelius never looked like the dancers. He certainly had the same fibers on, but he definitely didn't look like them. He kind of looked like the dad in the room. His suits, even though some of the dancers had on suits, weren't moving in quite the same ways. He was a little bit, I don't want to say stiff, but formal. There was a formality to him. He couldn't always mask that he wasn't a big fan of some of the guests on the show. I think every designer to some degree is influenced by what happened on *Soul Train*, even if you weren't born or you knew it ambiently. That was such a cultural zeitgeist of change, of new ideas, new momentum, it was really important. So whether you can trace your lines back to *Soul Train*, the veins are back into *Soul Train* for sure.

Lloyd Boston, who grew up in New Jersey and caught the show on the local New York station, noted that hair was an essential component of *Soul Train* style, especially the resplendent Afros of dancers and performers. "It was a leveling device that African Americans in the 1970s used to connect with each other," said the former Tommy Hilfiger art director and *The View* show regular.

Boston: Going back to the hair God gave you versus the hair that we're trying to create to assimilate . . . Almost like a halo. A crown. *Soul Train* became almost this living gallery of Afros— short, huge. Some were perfectly shaped. Some were picky. Some were short and red. Some were dyed. Some were wigs. I think that moment was so important because it showed you that anybody could do this. But if you look at some of the earlier episodes, you have to remember that 1972 looked very different from 1979. So in the earlier couple of years, you saw the kind of struggle between traditional black hair or natural black hair crossing paths with folks who had processed hair. You would see a few girls and guys with huge naturals, and then you would see a few girls and guys with processed hair. They all kind of coexisted together. So you saw girls who were trying to look like Marcia Brady next to girls that were trying to look like Angela Davis, and they were right there, whether they were in miniskirts or dashikis.

Like Oldham, Boston was taken by the boldness of the fashion choices, particularly by the male dancers. Boston suggested some of the dancers on the show were "embracing a slightly more effeminate style than you might see on the street . . . You would see guys on *Soul Train* wearing those skin-tight fishnet tank tops. You would see those spray-can-fit pants. You would say 'spray can' because you were proud to show your manhood at that time, and they would fit, and they would flair out at the bottom so you can move and groove and absolutely show the sexiness."

But, despite all the funky flair of the dancers, the show's host maintained his own, more dignified style of dress.

Boston: One thing you notice, though—Don Cornelius never touched that style. He was always respectable—almost an alderman, if you will. He looked like a community leader. His suits were always impeccable, though. When I think about his style, I remember his peaked lapels. Those hand-tied velvet bow ties. You know, it almost looked like prom pictures that we would see our parents or our older cousins wearing. His 'fro was always perfect. Those tinted glasses that would be like amber or mango. He would have some interesting shades.

A few of the female dancers, particularly Fawn Quinones, devised a mash-up of 1970s glam with iconic 1940s touches, very similar to what the female family vocal group the Pointer Sisters were working with. "So they kind of did this blend, this melding of vintage style," said Boston. "Shape cropped jackets with high-rolled shoulders. Back-seam stockings and platform Mary Janes. It was almost a take on the Andrews Sisters. Fawn would always carry an exotic fan, and her hair would be in rolls like an old switchboard operator in tight jackets and snug pencil skirts."

Black style, whether zoot suits in the 1940s or Afrocentric colors in the 1980s, have always had an impact on fashion around the globe. But in Boston's estimation, *Soul Train* has a special place as a style transmitter.

Boston: *Soul Train* is the first time our unique style expression was televised. The same way MTV launched punk and rock style in the 1980s, *Soul Train* did for black style in the 1970s. It may not have been in as many homes around the nation or around the world, but those trends were just made bigger than the album cover, bigger than the eight-track cassette label . . . You could take your cues: "I would love to try that. I need to layer a leather jacket over that. Oh my God, a dashiki with some culottes would be fantastic." It only takes one person to start a trend. The fact that these individuals who were expressing themselves, as teenagers do, could now reach millions of homes, they could inspire teenagers everywhere.

The peak of *Soul Train*'s fashion impact was those golden years of the seventies. With the rise of hip-hop and music videos in the eighties, a more casual, streetwise aesthetic would replace LA glitz, while videos would become the way new fashions would be communicated to young people. Still, today you can't think back to the seventies without visions of bell-bottoms and bushy Afros filling your mind.

Classic eighties fashion and hair.

DANCER PROFILE: Sam Solomon

Growing up in Fresno, California, a young man named Sam Solomon was a fan of 1960s dances like the jerk, the twist, and the flowing moves called the boogaloo. Sam also was a great observer of how people moved, be it a wino on the corner or a handicapped man with a distinctive walk. Giving himself the handle Boogaloo Sam, he moved down to Long Beach, California, in 1978. Along with his younger brother Popin' Pete Solomon, he formed a dance crew that included colorfully named Creepin' Sid, Puppet Boozer, Electric Boogaloo, and the Robot Dane. They called themselves the Electric Boogaloos.

What Sam created was a move he called popping. "Popping is flexing of the muscles in rhythm to the beat," Popin' Pete explained. "It's been given wrong names like pop locking, electric boogie, flexing, but it's just called poppin' because the original guys, they would do the moves, and they would just say 'Pop, Pop, Pop.' Just make that sound that they thought that this would be making if they could put sound effects on it. The boogaloo is more fluid. Poppin' is this hard-core move, where boogaloo is this groove dance."

The Electric Boogaloos began building a rep out in Long Beach at a recreation center known as the Hutch and a teen party called Noah's Ark. "Prior to poppin', everybody was just locking," Dane recalled. "When Sam came to Long Beach with his new style, it was almost like a gunfighter coming into town, and one by one he started turning out all the dancers. They would do their little thing and Sam would watch them. Sam would just—'Bam, bam, bam.' It was just like you're out of there. Quite a few of them totally just stopped dancing, period."

The crew, being naive and young (sixteen, seventeen years old), figured the best way to get discovered was to go dance on street corners on Hollywood Boulevard. The old Hollywood legend that movie siren Lana Turner was discovered at a lunch counter was very much alive in the imaginations of these young men. Today they'd post a YouTube video. Back in the 1970s, you had to find a way to catch someone's eye.

So the Electric Boogaloos hopped on a bus from Long Beach to downtown and then transferred to another bus, expecting to end up on the corner of Hollywood and Vine but ending up way across town in East LA. Instead of risking another bus mishap, they walked halfway across the city to Sunset and Doheny, and all along the way, "every time we saw a limo—it could have been a limo coming from a funeral or going to a prom—we would get on the corner and we would just start dancing," said Pete.

They were hanging by the bus stop at Sunset when a female dancer spotted them, came over, and asked them to explain some of their moves. Impressed, she passed their number to someone hiring dancers for shows at casino hotels in Lake Tahoe. The Electric Boogaloos got an audition and, like most LA street dancers of the era, were wearing gear that resembled that of the Lockers. The casting director's attitude was, according to Pete, "Oh, more lockers. I don't need more lockers for the show." But after watching them pop and boogaloo, the guys were hired to perform in Nevada for two months.

Everyone who spotted the Electric Boogaloos was immediately taken by their moves and either wanted to watch them or learn them. Quickly the popping style started to be adopted. New adherents added their own variations. An Electric Boogaloo member, Creepin' Sid, developed a move called the backslide. It looked like a man walking slowly backwards, defying physics and common sense. It was much admired and imitated by other dancers, though its mainstream debut as the moonwalk was years away.

Although their show-business career was off to an auspicious start, one form of validation the Electric Boogaloos sought was a chance to dance on *Soul Train*. "When we became a group, we said we haven't made it yet until we perform on *Soul Train*," said Pete. "That was true of any dancer coming up." Various members of the crew had auditioned for the show before and had been turned down.

The Electric Boogaloos' invitation to appear on the show resulted from the influence of popping. It had spread from the Bay Area to Long Beach and throughout Southern California. Two of *Soul Train*'s most popular dancers, Cash Cool and the Pop Along Kid—also known as Jeffrey Daniel—did a featured dance performance on the show that gave their interpretation of popping. Electric Boogaloo members Popin' Pete and Robot Dane were home watching the performance. When Cornelius asked the dancers about their moves, Cash Cool and Daniel told Cornelius this new style of movement was created by the Electric Boogaloos. Cornelius then turned to the camera and announced he'd soon be having the dance crew on the show.

Electric Boogaloo member Dane immediately got on the phone to *Soul Train*'s production office. "They were like, 'Oh my God, so happy you guys called.' They didn't really have a contact on us, and then no one had ever really asked us about trying to be on *Soul Train*. They had us come in and it was, like, wild."

Electric Boogaloo member Boozer said of the first show, "You have to remember when we performed on *Soul Train* the first time, Don was just going off word of mouth. He had never seen us perform. He had never seen a tape of us. Nothing. He had just seen what Jeff and Cash Cool did, and he had heard our name, but he had never seen us perform. So he pretty much booked us sight unseen."

The Electric Boogaloos would appear two times on *Soul Train*. In that first appearance, they each wore matching bright-colored suits (they called them skittle suits). Moreover, Cornelius would tell them something they'd later consider prophetic. Dane recalled, "Don said, 'You know what, I'm gonna give these guys credit for what they're doing before someone else comes along and tries to take credit for it and make a lot of money off it.'"

Cornelius spoke again about the group's impact years later, though he got some of the details wrong.

> **Cornelius:** Well, the first time we saw the moonwalk were some kids who called themselves Electric Boogaloo. And we got a tip that this was something very hot and very beautiful to see, and that we should try to get them on *Soul Train*, and we did. That is the first time that America—not just us, not just *Soul Train*—that *America* got exposed to the moonwalk. Now, anybody else who does the moonwalk, they learned most of it from Electric Boogaloo.

In 1983 Michael Jackson made a historic appearance on NBC's broadcast of *Motown 25*, a prime-time celebration of Berry Gordy's legendary record label. Though the show was packed with stars, it was Michael Jackson's performance of a dance the media labeled "the moonwalk" that was easily the evening's highlight. What few people know is the dance was created not by the musical superstar but out of the Electric Boogaloos. "What they call the moonwalk is not the moonwalk," Dane said. "It's the backslide. You know it's erroneous. The moonwalk actually looks like you're walking on the moon, like Marcel Marceau . . . Backsliding is you're going backwards. But we debuted that on *Soul Train* in 1979. When Michael does it on *Motown 25*, all of the sudden it was the moonwalk. So again, it was so important for us to do *Soul Train* because when you look at that and the Internet now, no one can say, 'Okay, you didn't do this.' That *Soul Train* performance sealed our fate in history."

The moves that the Electric Boogaloos introduced on *Soul Train* and elsewhere would inform the culture known as hip-hop, fuel several more quaint-looking eighties dance movies starring members of the crew, and allow the group to continue performing globally to this day.

DANCER PROFILE: Reggie Thornton

Reggie Thornton had two very different *Soul Train* tenures, separated by a decade and two cities. Raised in Gary, Indiana, during the early 1970s, Reggie was part of that original group that danced on the show during its early days in Chicago. Once *Soul Train* moved west, Thornton watched enviously from Indiana as the once-local show became a national phenomenon.

> **Thornton:** I used to watch [the LA show], seeing all the beautiful Afros, the beautiful people doing the beautiful dances, and the women and everyone looking great. I couldn't wait to come out here. I was hoping that Don Cornelius would send for us. But it never did happen. I just longed to get here. But it wasn't that easy. When I got out to California on July 15, 1980, I found out they were doing a taping of *Soul Train*. I heard they brought extra clothes, and you had to stand in line. So I found out they were taping at Metromedia studio in Hollywood. I had my suitcase in my hand as the gates opened, and I walked through the gates. I noticed

everyone was telling this gentleman, "Hey, how are you, Chuck?" Everybody's speaking to Chuck. So as I got in line, and I spoke to Chuck. I said, "Hey, how are you, Chuck?" And Chuck said, "Hey, who are you? Stand over here." So I stood over to the side. After a while everybody got in, and the gates closed, and I said, "Wait a minute! I'm supposed to be in there." Chuck said, "Well, this is a closed set." And I said, "I'm a Soul Trainer. I'm from Chicago!"

Don Cornelius had given us these cards that said "Soul Train Gang—Permanent Member of the Soul Train Gang." I showed Chuck this card, and he said, "What's that?" I said, "That's from Don Cornelius. He gave me this card and said I was a permanent *Soul Train* dancer." He said, "I've never seen that before," and went in the studio, and he closed the door. So maybe like a half hour went by, and I was so desperate to get in there I climbed the fence and I went inside the studio.

In the studio I saw all these people that I admired on television for all these years. I just thought it was the greatest thing. So I sat down for a while, and some song came on and the music got to me and I started dancing. All of a sudden Chuck Johnson noticed me out there. He said, "Excuse me. Can you come over here? What are you doing here?" I said, "I'm a *Soul Train* dancer from Chicago. I showed you my card." He told me to take a seat. I sat down and just watched everybody dance. I was excited and so full of anguish because I couldn't dance. I was just frustrated.

Toward the end of the day, Chuck let me come on the floor and start dancing. The next day, which was a Sunday, he let me in and I went to the back. I started dancing and they started doing the *Soul Train* line. That's the last thing they do at the end of the day. So when everyone lined up to be picked for the *Soul Train* line, Chuck saw me in the line, and he said, "No, you can't go down the *Soul Train* line." All the dancers, they were saying, "Oh, Chuck! He can dance. He can dance. Let him go down the line." Finally he let me have a shot. So I went down the *Soul Train* line, and they loved it. After that I came running down the *Soul Train* line every week.

While Thornton was a capable dancer, his greatest contribution to *Soul Train* lore involved a nondancing encounter with a pop diva. Episode #382 of the 1981–82 season was a tribute to Diana Ross timed to the release of her debut album on RCA Records, *Why Do Fools Fall in Love*, her first release after leaving Motown.

Thornton: I always thought that Diana Ross was very sexy. I don't know whether she was a cougar or not, whether she was into young men or not. I always thought she was sexy as a young child. So they did a segment where they had a question-and-answer period. And I had a question for Diana, and my question was, "Diana, everybody who knows me knows that you're my favorite star, and there's one thing I've always wanted to do. I've always wanted to kiss you on nationwide television, can I have that opportunity?" And she said, "Oh, yes, you can do it." So I went up to Diana and I kissed her, and she said, "Oh, yeah," and she hugs real tight too. That was her response. And when all my friends back home saw that, they said, I can't believe you kissed Diana Ross!

Chapter 8
WHITES ON *SOUL TRAIN*

DON CORNELIUS was at a posh private party in Los Angeles in the 1970s when he ran into Hall of Fame quarterback Joe Namath. Broadway Joe, who'd won a Super Bowl with the New York Jets, was ending his career as a gimpy-kneed veteran with the then Los Angeles Rams.

When Namath was introduced to Cornelius, the quarterback said, "Yeah, I know Don Cornelius. He does the *Soul Train* show"—which is a testament to how well-known the show was among white Americans.

But then the conversation took a turn. "How come you don't let white people on that show?" he asked Don, who replied, "Well, Joe, we've always had white people on the show."

Namath was not convinced. "No, I've seen your show, you don't allow white people to be on the show."

By this time, the quarterback was getting a little aggressive with Don and, weak-kneed or not, Namath was still a six-foot-three pro athlete whom Don didn't want any trouble with. So Don asked, "Well,

Joe, do you watch *Soul Train* every week?" Namath told him he didn't. Now Don had him.

"Well," Don replied, "the week you don't watch it, that's when the white people are there." Before Namath could reply, Don had moved on. This comical exchange reflected the perception that many people, mostly white, thought that *Soul Train* consciously excluded whites from the premises. While white dancers were never excluded from the show, none became as famous as Asian dancer Cheryl Song. Don could be very expansive on white dancers and the stereotype about their absence of rhythm.

Cornelius: For as long as I can remember, there was always at least a few white dancers, all of whom [could] always hold their own with the black dancers. I'm not a believer in the myth that says white people cannot dance because it's been proven to me over the years that they can. The difference is we, as black people, start dancing at age two. Our parents are saying, "Come on, baby, let's do this." You start dancing as a toddler, and you learn that you must keep time with the music or else your parents will challenge you to do so. A lot of white people don't get that kind of coaching. We've experienced situations where a white dancer was not keeping time with the music, and we explained to them that this is a requirement: "You must keep time with the music." They kept time just like anybody else, but if nobody ever told them to do it, then very often they couldn't.

Correcting a lack of rhythm may not be as easy as Don suggests, but let's give him the benefit of the doubt. Any white kid who'd made it onto the floor at *Soul Train* must have been capable of keeping a beat. Truth is, no white dancer made an deep impact on the show, but the appearances of white musicians, particularly in *Soul Train*'s early years, live large in the show's mythology.

There is a trio of white performers on *Soul Train* that are usually regarded as "pioneers." Gino Vannelli, Elton John, and David Bowie are not only white but non-American: Vannelli is Canadian, John and Bowie both British. Around 1975, the Average White Band, almost all Scots, also made a memorable appearance.

The first white American acts on *Soul Train* were instrumentalists, not singers, which probably explains why they aren't well remembered. Dennis Coffey, once a top session guitarist for Motown in Detroit, began recording R&B instrumental tracks and had a million-selling single, the driving "Scorpio," in 1971. (The B-side, "Sad Angel," is a personal favorite of mine.) Coffey performed "Scorpio" on episode #15.

The second white collective on the show was the Bay Area jazz-rock collective Tower of Power, fronted by black vocalist Lenny Williams. Tower of Power taped episode #79 during the 1973–74 season, sharing the broadcast with two vocal groups, the Pointer Sisters and Tavares.

Band leader and tenor saxophonist Emilio Castillo recalled that appearance with great affection.

Castillo: We had hit a place in our career where we were on the charts and getting really popular. We had done *Midnight Special, In Concert,* and *New Year's Rockin' Eve*—all those kinds of shows. But to be on *Soul Train* was really the thing. Tower of Power was first and foremost a soul band. We come from the Oakland side of the Bay, where there are all kinds of people. We never thought about being a white soul band. We're in front of the Soul Train Gang, and Don Cornelius is towering over us and asking these questions in that big, deep voice . . . But as soon as we hit that downbeat, man we were right in there . . . We hit a real hard groove, and I remember we did this one song called "To Say the Least, You're the Most." He came down off the stage, and my singer Lenny Williams was singing, and the horn section was following him, and we cut through the Soul Train Gang and walked right out of the studio. That's how it faded to commercial. It was really cool.

While Tower of Power's appearance is now somewhat obscure, Gino Vannelli's performance on episode #128 in February 1975 is a signature moment for so many viewers. The Canadian is kind of the Jackie Robinson of white singers when it comes to *Soul Train*. He arrived on the show from the unlikely soul music mecca of Montreal, Canada.

Vannelli claimed that "the club scene in Montreal in the mid-sixties, you would think you were in Harlem. You know it was really deep R&B. They had the esoteric Isaac Hayes records when they weren't out yet. All those seven-minute records. Everybody wanted to emulate that. Everyone was listening to Little Anthony, and all those groups you know in Montreal in the mid-sixties. I was lucky I was brought up with that, and I had that sense of rhythm and that sense of, well, American soul that you didn't find anywhere else but America. It was a real strong influence on my life."

That influence was also reflected in Vannelli's hair. Though he was Italian, Vannelli sported a circular Afro as recognizable as his resonant vocals.

The handsome singer with the emotive tenor voice signed in 1973 with A&M Records, one of the classier boutique labels of the era, which was owned by Jerry Moss and trumpeter Herb Alpert, who himself had a number of hits on his own in the early 1960s ("The Lonely Bull," "A Taste of Honey"). The Los Angeles–based label had a strong roster that included Billy Preston, the Carpenters, Cat Stevens, Quincy Jones, and later the Brothers Johnson and the Police.

Tower of Power was the first predominantly white act to play on *Soul Train*.

Vannelli remembered: "Herb is one of the original guys who shot from the hip, because he just intuitively knew what he liked and what a lot of other people would like. He didn't have to go through committees and put you through the hoops that a lot of record companies would today. He just sort of heard and said, Yeah."

At A&M, Vannelli was very much a small fish in a big pond. His first album, *Crazy Life*, didn't do well, but the label gave him a second shot. While recording his *Powerful People* album, Vannelli was living at a hotel on Sunset Boulevard called the Hallmark. Sitting in his hotel room, he heard someone singing a familiar melody outside by the pool. It was a song from his debut album.

Vannelli: So I went out into the pool area, and there was Stevie
Wonder singing "Granny Goodbye," from the *Crazy Life* album. His
brother introduced me to him, and of course I was in awe, and we
kind of struck up a relationship, and Stevie asked me to play on his
tour. He just thought it would be right. I did seven or eight concerts
with Stevie, and it really changed my life and changed my career. I
thought all musics were valid, and I just so happened to love R&B.
I didn't want to be one of those white guys trying to have a black
sound, because [then] I always sound so loungy and stupid. But I
would always let that kind of music affect my music. Rhythmically,
perhaps harmonically. I really wanted to mix a little R&B with an
Italian bel canto style of singing. It took me a little while to develop,
but that's what came out. Your style is nothing more than your
limitations. I remember having a conversation with Stevie: "Are you
sure you really want me to do this? It could be my death, and maybe
it's not such a good thing for you." He said, "I think the audience
will like you." So we opened in Cincinnati, and I was just scared. My
knees knocking. But everywhere we went we were getting standing
ovations. Stevie would come onstage and say wasn't it great, and you
can buy his record, and da-da-da. I was amazed with that. And within
a few months, we did *Soul Train*, and that's when I could go out on
my own. So it was a life-turning, or at least a career-turning, event
for me. And the fact that I could play to such an integrated audience
at that time—I don't think many people were doing that. Maybe the
hair helped a little bit. The 'fro was a big thing in those days.

It's a little unclear how Vannelli was booked on the show. Don
told VH1 that Vannelli's folks asked for a shot, while the singer suggests that *Soul Train* invited him on. No matter who made the first
move, opening for Stevie Wonder is probably what put the relatively
obscure Vannelli on the show's radar.

Vannelli: For me it wasn't a cultural phenomenon or anything like that until later. It was just a show, and they said you'll be the first white guy on the show. I said, Okay, yeah, I'll do it. Is it good for ratings? Is it good. Can I get further ahead? They said, Yeah, yeah, you can just do it. I didn't want to lip-synch the record. It was almost a live performance. We went back into the studio and we tweaked things and left some things out so we could perform to [the track] live. The conversation with Don was very amicable, but for me it wasn't this cultural revelation until maybe a couple years later when people started saying, "You know, you're the first white person on *Soul Train*." I said, "Really? Does it mean something?" Of course it meant something if I could cross those boundaries. Because in the coming years, right after *Soul Train*, my audiences were—I wouldn't say predominantly, but at least 50 percent black. Every time I went to play Atlanta and Dallas and Chicago and Pittsburgh, it was very—a very mixed audience, but I would say at least 40 or 50 percent black. I would say it had some impact.

Vannelli, like many folks on first meeting Cornelius, was a little unsure how to relate to the imposing TV host. "You know at first, it was a little bit stiff relationship, because I think he wanted to say the right things," said the singer, "and I wanted to say the right things. As time wore on, we kind of got a little closer, and I remember—this is a long time ago—I remember I asked him, 'Why did you invite me on the show? I'm obviously not a black artist.' He said, 'Well, I consider you off-white.'"

Unlike Vannelli, who was just starting his career, the next two white performers on *Soul Train* were already huge pop stars. By 1971

Elton John was a hit-making machine and the first artist since the Beatles to have four albums in the Billboard Top Ten simultaneously. John was in the middle of an incredible run of success in which he'd have seven consecutive No. 1 albums. He had an outrageous sense of visual humor, reflected in his hundreds of pairs of glasses (some with windshield wipers) and his pianos.

David Bowie was a rock icon who'd built his reputation with hooky rock singles and an ever-shifting stage persona. He'd been a star of the glitter rock movement that emphasized sexual ambiguity, rocking guitar riffs, and flamboyant stage shows. Way before rappers adopted personas who donned different identities, he led the way by being first Ziggy Stardust and later the Thin White Duke. Each time, he also altered his musical direction.

Both Elton John and David Bowie were huge figures in the very white world of pop and rock radio, and both asked to be on *Soul Train*.

"This wasn't salesmanship on our part with Elton John or David Bowie. We didn't pursue that," Don said. "They just called up one day, and it was like, Elton John wants to do *Soul Train*, and we were like, Fine! It just worked out where they were admiring something about what we were doing and decided that, being the free spirits that they were, there's no reason why we're not doing this. It ushered in another kind of growth period when major white recording stars elected themselves to do *Soul Train*."

Elton John was very much a pop artist. He, along with his lyricist and writing partner Bernie Taupin, wrote tunes in any style (hard rock, English music hall, folk, country, honky-tonk) while also anchoring them with vibrant melodies. R&B was not their strong suit, although they would compose a fun tribute to the Philly sound, "Philadelphia Freedom," that John performed on *Soul Train*.

Pop superstar Elton John made a landmark performance of "Bennie and the Jets" on *Soul Train*

But the song that put John on the black audience's radar is perhaps the oddest hit of his career. "Bennie and the Jets," a song from the hugely successful *Goodbye Yellow Brick Road* album. If John had had his way, it shouldn't have even been a single. The song, written from the point of view of a fan watching a concert by a band called Bennie and the Jets, was not a typical subject for a big single. To buttress the lyric, crowd noises, taken from John's live shows and a bit of Jimi Hendrix's at the Isle of Wight festival, were laid over the vocals. The rhythm was kind of a stiff strut built around a choppy piano riff. John sings with a lot of energy and some falsetto, but very few people actually understand the words other than the chorus of "Bennie! Bennie! Bennie and the Jets!"

Still, this odd assortment of elements came together and had real appeal to black listeners. My sister Andrea, a huge soul music fan who had no interest in (and often contempt for) pop music, spent the summer of 1974 singing Taupin's hook, symbolic of the fact that "Bennie" would go to No. 1—not just on the pop chart but on the R&B chart too—and sell 2.8 million 45s. The fact that Andrea didn't really know the rest of the lyrics, save a word or two, spoke to the appealing power of its musical elements—Elton's piano and the jerky, funky rhythm.

Watching the performance now, with John wearing a bedazzled green bowler hat with matching green suit and one of his many glittering, customized pairs of glasses, pounding away at a clear plastic piano, you can tell he's totally jazzed to be there. Near the fade of "Bennie," he freestyles a bit, egging on the dancers to join in. John, always a dynamic entertainer, seems electrified by the vibe in the room, resulting in a truly fun musical moment.

Theoretically, David Bowie's appearance on episode #165 should be discussed next, but before Bowie another group from the United Kingdom broke the *Soul Train* color line. The Average White Band from Scotland, students of Motown, Stax, and soul music of all kinds, would develop into an above-average funk collective. The original members met while attending university in Dundee, Scotland's fourth-largest city, where they were part of a soul-music-loving scene not dissimilar to the one captured in Roddy Doyle's novel (and the movie) *The Commitments*, about a similar soul scene in Dublin. Formed in 1972 by bassist Alan Gorrie and rhythm guitarist Onnie McIntyre, this tight six-piece band would eventually get signed to the classic soul label Atlantic Records, where, under the guidance of producer Arif Mardin, they'd cut a series of excellent 1970s albums.

Then there was David Bowie. Todd Oldham recalls that Bowie's appearance "was really a shock. Because, well, first of all, he didn't look too much like the other performers in any world, but certainly not on *Soul Train* . . . Well, he was so genuinely unusual, I think there was no reference point to assimilate David Bowie. It was kind of like you're going eighty miles an hour in a convertible. You didn't know what you were seeing."

While Bowie had recorded his first eight albums as an androgynous glam rocker, on his ninth album he was inspired to create "plastic soul," his take on the Sound of Philadelphia that was dominating dance floors in Europe as well as the United States. In the fall of 1974, Bowie camped out at Sigma Sound Studios in the City of Brotherly Love to record the bulk of his *Young Americans* album. The title cut was clearly influenced by watching Cornelius's show, with punning lyrical references to "Afro-Shelias" and "blacks got respect and whites got his soul train." During the sessions, the British singer became impressed with the voice and songwriting of Luther Vandross, a young New Yorker singing background vocals. Later they would take a song Vandross had previously recorded on one of his Atlantic solo albums and rewrite it, calling the new version "Fascination" and including it on *Young Americans*.

"Fame," a No. 1 single that was the last track on *Young Americans*, was actually recorded in New York's Electric Ladyland Studio, which had been opened by the late guitarist Jimi Hendrix. That record, which featured a fuzzy guitar riff and a down-tempo, oddly syncopated rhythm track, was cowritten by ex-Beatle John Lennon and displayed Lennon's usual quality of experimentation and pop success. And it was this track that would be Bowie's natural gateway onto *Soul Train*. Gone was the glitter. In its place was a pale blue suit and yellow shirt with a large collar. Bowie was entering the Thin White Duke phase of his career, when a more elegant and dressy soul aesthetic would define him. This appearance on *Soul Train* would be his introduction of this new direction.

As noted earlier, Don's interviews could often be awkward. But his chat with Bowie was unusually stiff, as the singer seemed a bit intimidated to be on the show. Cornelius may have unnerved Bowie, and that may have caused the dancers asking the singer questions to seem uncomfortable as well. Usually there was a giddy, excited quality to the interaction between the dancers and singers, but this felt strained. An interview Bowie did in 2000 with the BBC about his poor performances of "Fame" and "Golden Years" on *Soul Train* explains his behavior.

Bowie: I do remember not knowing the . . . the words. I wasn't even buoyant enough to feel apologetic or . . . I mean, I really was a little shit in that way! I hadn't bothered to learn it. And the MC of the show, who is a really charming guy, took me on one side after the third or fourth take where I just had no idea what the lyrics were, and he said, "Do you know there are kids lined up to do this show, who have fought their whole lives to try and get a record and come on here?" And—and it made no . . . I know now, looking back, but at the time, it made no impression. His little speech to me, which was absolutely necessary . . . and I just screwed up the lyrics. I mean, I haven't even seen the show for years, so I can't even remember if it looked like I screwed it up . . . But I think maybe I wrote them out in the end and read them off a card or something . . . which I must say I now do all the time!

Though lackluster, Bowie's appearance was still a landmark for the show and, likely, whetted the appetite of a slew of 1980s British pop rockers to come on the show, something that would become unexpectedly and increasingly commonplace.

For all the fascination with white pop stars deciding to cross over to black television, there is one Caucasian singer for whom appearing on *Soul Train* was never a big deal. Mary Christine Brockert, known professionally as Teena Marie, released her debut album, *Wild and*

Peaceful, on Motown Records in 1979 with the production and writ-ing assistance of funk master Rick James. Her debut album didn't have the petite brunette's picture on the cover. It had a seascape, a Motown precaution to prevent the white singer from being prejudged by black audiences.

Once black folks heard Marie's music, her color didn't matter. "Teena Marie was, for many people, an honorary black person," said scholar-author Tricia Rose, "you know, a black person trapped in a white girl's body. Nobody saw Teena Marie in my circles as a white woman somehow interloping or trying to act like she was soul-ful. She's not performing in a fake way. She is just an extraordinary singer, and her personal integrity comes through, so Teena Marie makes perfect sense. There was no sense of 'Who is this white girl on *Soul Train*?'"

Marie made her debut in episode #308 of the 1979–80 season alongside her mentor Rick James. She would become a regular, appearing four more times over the next five years and in a total of ten episodes during her productive career. Her ease with black folks came from growing up in Venice, California, in an area called Dog-town, best known as the home of a rebel group of skaters, Z-Boys, who'd become X Games legends.

While growing up in Venice, she had Mexican and black and surfer friends while obsessing over Smokey Robinson songs and watching *Soul Train*. "You know, I never really imagined that I would grow up to perform on the same stage with the Whispers or Al Green, and now I sing with Al Green," she said. After showing vocal skills in a couple of bands, Marie met veteran Motown producer Hal Davis, who'd worked with the Jackson Five. Berry Gordy himself signed her, but it took several failed recording attempts before she and Rick James clicked. On her first *Soul Train* appearance, Marie performed the up-tempo "Sucker for Love" and the mid-tempo "Don't Look Back."

Teena Marie: I remember I had this pink butterfly costume on, and it had pink butterfly wings when I put my hands out. I was really, really excited to be on TV and have my people loving my music. [Performing on *Soul Train*] was really important because there wasn't a lot of shows for us, you know? My skin is white, but I'm not looked at like that. I'm a black entertainer and always have been very, very proud of my history and who I am. I didn't get played on a lot of white stations. I only had one crossover record in my whole career. It's because of black people that I am who I am . . . Black people had always embraced me and supported me as their own. It was never looked at as a black or white thing. Black people love good music, right?

Her favorite *Soul Train* performance occurred in 1988 when she performed her classic ballad "Ooo La La La" with choreography by her best friend, Mickey Boyce-Ellis, and backing vocals by two of the Mary Jane Girls. Grooving around the stage in intensely teased blondish-brunette hair and a tight black dress with see-through sections, Marie displays her soaring vocals while singing one of her self-penned love songs. With "Ooo La La La," as with so many of her compositions, Marie manages to be girlishly romantic yet wisely adult.

After her extraordinary debut, Marie would record several superb albums for Motown, including her masterful *It Must Be Magic* in 1981, which includes her biggest R&B hit, "Square Biz." Her tenure with Motown ended badly with a contract dispute in 1982. She recorded for CBS's Epic Records from 1983 to 1990 and had her biggest pop single, "Lovergirl," but seemed pressured to abandon her soul roots and saw her sales falter. While hip-hop producers sampled her work throughout the 1990s and into the twenty-first century, Marie's output of new music slowed, though there were gems on every album she released.

In November 2010, she suffered a grand mal epileptic seizure. Then, on December 26, 2010, she was found unconscious at her home. The LA county coroner concluded that Teena Marie died of natural causes.

DANCER PROFILE: Crystal McCarey

Crystal McCarey was one of the great beauties to grace the *Soul Train* dance floor, a woman who counted among her fans the Jackson Five and Marvin Gaye. These days she makes jewelry and sells it on her website, but from 1975 until the mid-1980s, she sparkled like a diamond herself. Yet life for this lean, lovely, fair-skinned lady was far from charmed. She grew up in *Soul Train*'s hometown of Chicago and lived her early years relatively privileged, but then her family "wound up having to live on the verge of poverty for quite a while," McCarey said.

In the 1950s, Crystal's mother, Barbara, was a showgirl and part of a revue of dancers selected to perform at Las Vegas's Moulin Rouge Hotel, Sin City's first black-owned entertainment establishment, which opened in 1955. That opening was an extremely noteworthy event: *Life* magazine documented it by putting a photograph of Barbara McCarey on its cover, and a *Las Vegas Sun* photo from May 1955 shows Barbara McCarey and six Moulin Rouge showgirls posed backstage in feathered tops, black skirts, and light-colored stockings. All are lovely, but Barbara's large eyes, full lips, dark black hair, and thin, athletic build stand out and forecast her daughter's future beauty. While the Moulin Rouge opened with great optimism, the enterprise was dogged by racism and never really took off. The casino hotel would burn down in 1957.

In the aftermath of that disappointment, Barbara McCarey "became a kept woman for a number of years, and we lived, like I said, very well," her daughter said. "When that situation fizzled out, she did make some bad decisions, and she paid a very, very heavy price by having a stroke at the age of thirty-two . . . My mother was in a wheelchair. She lost complete control of the left side of her body. So she went from being a phenomenal dancer to being in a wheelchair." Then her family ended up living in Chicago public housing, and it was during this sad period that *Soul Train* took on new meaning for Crystal.

> **McCarey:** I would say that *Soul Train* impacted young people in poverty. For that hour, they weren't getting into trouble. They weren't stealing. They weren't robbing people. After that one hour, they still felt positive and felt good about themselves. They kind of held that from week to week. When I was watching *Soul Train* in Chicago, I had no idea at all that I would ever come to California, that I would ever be on the show. But I think it had a strong impact on young urban women in terms of grooming and the way they took care of themselves.

Barbara—who became known to their neighbors in the projects as "Miss Bobby"—was determined that her oldest daughter not be trapped in poverty, so she began calling old friends in Los Angeles. "Even at that point, in her sorrow and feeling the pain she felt for her own self, she saved my life and got me out of the projects," McCarey said.

A family friend sent the young woman a ticket to California and helped her find a place to stay. After growing up in the Chicago cold, Crystal immediately took to the Los Angeles sun. She landed a job as a receptionist at a law firm and was walking down an LA street on lunch break when her life changed again. A car pulled up next to her and began driving alongside her. A black man leaned out of his window checking her out. Unfortunately for a woman like McCarey, this was an unwanted but not unusual experience.

"I'm just looking at him, and I'm like, Okay, I know he

doesn't think I'm getting in that car," she recalled. "Finally he pulled over and said, 'Excuse me! Excuse me! Look, I'm not trying to pick you up. I don't mean you any harm. Can you dance?'" The man handed her his card. It turned out to be *Soul Train*'s Chuck Johnson. To make this even more Hollywood, McCarey says this all happened across the street from *Soul Train*'s offices. So after work she went over to meet with Don Cornelius himself.

"He was sitting behind this huge, imposing desk. He didn't have a lot to say, 'cause Don was just so cool. He looked at me and said, 'Yeah, she's cute.' Then Chuck said, 'Okay, so this is it. This is your shot now. Whatcha got.' He put on some music, and I just started dancing, and that was it. He said, 'Okay, you did all right, kid.' They gave me the information for the taping, and I probably didn't sleep a night between that audition and the two weeks I had to wait for the taping. I did the first taping, and they told me they wanted me back. What that did for my mother, in that wheelchair, living in the projects, to be able to see me dancing every week, I have no words."

Chapter 9

DISCO FEVER

|||||||||||||||||||||||||||||||||||

THE RISE of dance music called disco—named for its popularity at the growing number of discotheques around the nation—became the hottest musical fad starting in 1974 and peaking three years later. Musically, disco took liberally from the sophisticated soul sounds of Philly International Records and Barry White, styles that took the rough edges off R&B, maintaining funk underneath a rich, orchestral tapestry of strings and horns. From 1973 to 1975, the *Soul Train* theme song, "TSOP (The Sound of Philadelphia)," was definitely one of the songs that inspired the disco movement. Over time the sound of disco would evolve, with lesser hands turning the innovations of the Philly Sound and White into bland formula, while keyboard-driven European dance music, or Euro disco, rhythmically flattened out the sound.

But disco was about more than music. It gave license for white people to couples-dance to pop music for the first time since the rock revolution of the late 1960s. Out went tie-dyed shirts, unruly hair, and shaking awkwardly to guitar solos. In were platform shoes, upscale fashions, and cocaine. The hustle, a touch dance with elements of Latin salsa and traditional ballroom, became the first dance associated with disco.

This combination of music and dance, which awakened a generation of white Americans to the pleasures of the dance floor, generated scores of dance shows—both on local television and in syndication—but *Soul Train* survived in large part because it was already way ahead of the dance-music curve. Though crafty white groups like the Bee Gees prospered by exploiting discomania, many of the musical acts featured on *Soul Train* were already making tracks being played at discos. While disco definitely sucked a lot of soul out of popular black music, it didn't diminish *Soul Train*. In some ways, it helped the show.

Cornelius: Well, the key ingredient for the success of *Soul Train* was that it's very solidly based on black music. These were the best dance records made for our beginning period, our second decade, our third decade, and any future decades. The best dance records made during those periods were black records. Made by black artists, black singers, black musicians. The best dance music was our folks, okay? And it took us to a point of decision when disco evolved. We didn't know whether to join the bandwagon and say this is a *Soul Train* disco show. We didn't know what to do, because disco came in strong. It was intimidating. And we came to realize that the best disco records, the very best, invariably— almost invariably—were black records. And so we made a commitment to just play the best black records we could find, during the disco era or not, and we remained okay. We just played the best dance records possible. You want to call it disco, fine. I'm playing the best dance records I can find, and most of the best disco records, if not all of them, were actually black records.

Disco would have a variety of impacts on black music. While rawer-sounding records never went away (with bands like Parliament-Funkadelic, Slave, the Bar-Kays, and Cameo staying true to the funk), the sophisticated sounds of disco were viewed by many record-industry executives as an easier way to reach white audiences. Some R&B stars found success adapting to disco flavor (Johnnie Taylor's "Disco Lady" in 1976 was the biggest hit of his long career), while many great talents made their worst records chasing the trend. (Aretha Franklin's 1979 album *La Diva* was her poorest-selling record ever.)

Disco also introduced a number of new acts to *Soul Train*. A few, like the New York–based band Chic, would have staying power. But most were one- or two-hit wonders (the Trammps, South Shore Commission, First Choice) who never sold many records outside the East Coast. More enduring was the impact disco would have on dancing on the show, as the hustle began sharing the dance floor with popping and locking. The long-legged individuality that dancers like Damita Jo Freeman had introduced to the show wouldn't go away, but less funky, more self-conscious sophistication in movement and dress became part of the weekly mix. *Soul Train* was never overrun by the faux glitz of *Saturday Night Fever*, but dance culture was changing, and the show reflected that evolution.

But Don Cornelius would do more than accommodate disco acts on his show. He'd use disco as a springboard into his own label by plucking a couple of stars off his dance floor.

Chapter 10

JODY AND JEFFREY
(AND O'BRYAN)

||||||||||||||||||||||||||||||||

THERE IS no question that Don Cornelius is the most important figure to emerge from *Soul Train*. It was his idea, and his on-camera personality and off-camera decisions shaped the show. But the next three most important people in the show's history are two dancers and a businessman, folks who actually made their biggest mark after they left the show. And all three of them did it together, capitalizing on an opportunity that eluded Don.

Jeffrey Daniel and Jody Watley were the coolest kids to grace *Soul Train*'s soundstage, while Dick Griffey was a behind-the-scenes force who would become one of the most important music moguls of the 1970s and 1980s. All would make their marks with a label called SOLAR Records, a company Cornelius helped found.

Back in 1971, Daniel and his family lived close to Denker Playground, where *Soul Train* was holding auditions, but Daniel was an adolescent then and knew nothing about the show. His real introduction to *Soul Train* happened after his mother relocated with him to Grand Rapids, Michigan, where on Saturdays, while munching on his morning cereal, he watched it religiously.

"I was a dancer, and I always did love dancing and music," Daniel said. "Just to see these young black kids giving fun and just grooving. It was amazing. I'm watching *Soul Train* every week, and I was wondering, 'Wait a minute. If *Soul Train* is in LA, why am I here?'"

Daniel wasn't doing well in high school, so he borrowed money and hopped a plane back to Cali. As discussed in Tyrone Proctor's dancer profile, Daniel began hanging out at Maverick's Flat, where he became part of Tyrone Proctor's crew and also witnessed Don Campbell's locking innovations. Initially his dance partner was his older sister Joyce. Then he began dancing with a young woman he knew from church named Jody Watley.

During *Soul Train*'s early years, Jody and her family were living in Chicago and were dedicated viewers. "The dancers were really the stars of the show," Watley said. "I had favorite dancers—Pat Davis, Tyrone Proctor, Sharon Hill, Little Joe Chism. I remember writing fan letters to them, asking, 'How do you get on the show?' So it was definitely very impactful for me. I had no idea that at some point my parents would end up moving to Los Angeles. It ended up being a twist of fate."

Reverend John Watley had been a very popular DJ in Chicago, broadcasting gospel music on Sundays on WVON. Apparently he and Cornelius knew each other, but according to Jody, neither man was fond of the other. Through his radio contacts, John Watley made a slew of show-business friends: R&B star Jackie Wilson would be named his daughter's godfather, Johnnie Taylor was a close friend, and Sam Cooke an occasional employer. At some point, however, John Watley lost his church, which instigated the family's move west.

The minute adolescent Jody Watley arrived in LA, she was obsessed with getting on *Soul Train*. But she had no contacts in Los Angeles and was living in the Jungle, a notorious ghetto housing complex off Crenshaw Boulevard, miles from Hollywood geographically and centuries away mentally. (The Jungle was featured prominently in the film *Training Day*.)

One day, while riding in the car with her mother, Watley spotted Tyrone Proctor walking on Stocker Avenue. Suddenly the fourteen-year-old shouted, "Stop the car!," bolted out onto the sidewalk, and ran up to the famous dancer. She introduced herself and tried to get him to tell her where *Soul Train* was, how to get on the show. Proctor was polite and wary, slipping away from the excited girl before he really told her anything useful.

The next weekend in church, a young man named Bobby Washington approached Watley and asked, "Would you be interested in being my partner on *Soul Train*?" Washington's regular partner was out of town, and he (rightly) thought Watley had a great look. "So he ended up being my way in," Watley said.

For her first show, she wore a crocheted hat and high-waisted yellow pants, but she doesn't remember much about that first time on set other than being told to take off the hat. There was a no-hats-on-the-show rule.

What she does recall is wanting to get back on *Soul Train*.

Watley: This can't be the Cinderella, and my-carriage-turns-into-a-pumpkin moment. So then my journey on *Soul Train* got really interesting. It took me many months of taking the bus up to the tapings and trying to weave my way in the line. There would be a security guard. He would check off the names. So I would ride the bus back home, and I would cry and come back the next month and try again.

Daniel knew other members of Watley's family before they'd met, but once they'd been introduced he immediately took a liking to this lean, large-eyed young woman.

> **Daniel:** At one point I started coming to Jody's place after school. She was still in high school. We would practice dance routines either at her place or at the choir director's house. We had chemistry because we skated well together.

Daniel and Watley used to skate at the Hollywood Roller Bowl, developing a rhythm and moves that would be reflected on *Soul Train*. "It wasn't contrived. It just happened. It was very natural."

Watley, along with Daniel, Cleveland Moses Jr., Sharon Hill, and others, would become part of the waacking dancers crew that was centered around Proctor. "I think we all just had a common love for what we were doing," Daniel said. "We would sometimes dress alike, all four of us. Or just Tyrone would be with Sharon, and I would be with Jody."

Very quickly, Jody and Jeffrey became their own entity. Whether they were on a riser, in the middle of the dance floor, or grooving down the *Soul Train* line, the camera loved them both. For one show, they incorporated a fake fight into their dance. Watley said, "That was inspired from an actual real fight that had happened on the show between a couple of dancers who were very popular but didn't care for each other." Recalling their days at the roller rink, the duo once skated down the line. Jeffrey even brought two unicycles to the set. At another taping, they used balloons as props. "We were very theatrical with it," said Watley. Charlie Chaplin, Danny K, and mimes Shields and Yarnell were all influences on Daniel and Watley.

Cynthia Horner made them regular *Right On!* magazine pinups, with Jody emerging as a late-1970s style icon. She could rock silver lamé pants and red-glitter Converse sneakers, vintage 1940s-inspired dresses with pumps or her prom dress. Her hair was an ongoing adventure, sometimes filled with tons of ribbons, sometimes with a long ponytail or a 1940s hairdo. (When I produced Chris Rock's documentary *Good Hair*, we used a Jody Watley video to illustrate the range of black hairstyles.)

But soon Jody learned that this kind of celebrity did not come without its costs. Watley became a target—both at *Soul Train* and at school.

Watley: I can think of some outfits that I wore on *Soul Train*, some of the dancers would say, "What's she wearing? What does she think she's doing?" *Soul Train* was very competitive, and there was a lot of what they'd call hateration now. You had a lot of that. That would go on at school, too. I could wear something to school that I thought was cool, and kids would laugh at me, run me home. You know, it never really dissuaded me from liking the things that I liked. I'm still the same way. So that sort of thing is just a part of you. You just kind of have to be fearless. Not really minding if you might be ridiculed for wearing something. You're not afraid to be who you really are.

By the time Jody Watley had been on the show for three years, she'd blossomed from a skinny fourteen-year-old to a stylish seventeen-year-old—and her dance partner, Jeffrey Daniel, was easily the most identifiable male dancer on *Soul Train*. They were primed to take their careers to the next level. So was a man named Dick Griffey.

Griffey was a big, bold, sometimes intimidating man with a strong presence, a vision of the future, and a great eye for talent. Born in

1938 and raised in a Nashville housing project, Griffey developed an interest in drumming and built a rep as a musician by playing local clubs before briefly attending the black college Tennessee State University, then enlisting in the navy.

Once out of the military service, Griffey moved to LA in the mid-1960s and resumed his interest in music, becoming part owner of the Guys and Dolls nightclub, where he developed a network of contacts in the music business and built a reputation as a solid citizen in the sometimes shifty business of booking and concert promotion. One of his partners in Guys and Dolls was basketball player Dick Barnett, a college star at Tennessee A&I in Nashville (now Tennessee State), who'd go on to play for the Los Angeles Lakers and, later, on two championship New York Knicks teams in 1970 and 1973. Another member of Griffey's Guys and Dolls team was Chuck Johnson, who'd be a close business associate for some forty years. He'd later work on *Soul Train* as a talent scout who both found dancers and worked as a liaison between them and Cornelius.

Dick Griffey's production company became a force in the LA music business at a time when black music's audiences were expanding and R&B shows were moving from midsize venues to arenas like Inglewood's Great Western Forum. Looking for new challenges, Griffey became a talent coordinator for *Soul Train* and helped Cornelius press big-name acts to give the show a chance. By the mid-seventies, with *Soul Train* established, Cornelius and Griffey wanted to find ways to capitalize on their new power. In 1975 they founded Soul Train Records, which was distributed by RCA Records. They weren't a power in R&B, but they were trying to build their presence in a deal brokered by Cornelius's longtime benefactor Clarence Avant. To emphasize the brand connection, the first act they signed was called the Soul Train Gang.

"They put out an audition for a Soul Train Gang singing group," Daniel said. "And I did the audition. It must have been horrible, because I was playing the keyboard and trying to sing [Major Harris's] 'Love Won't Let Me Wait' at the same time, and they said get out of here . . . A lot of the dancers were disappointed because they felt that they had been *Soul Train* dancers for so long, and here comes an opportunity, and they just picked people who had nothing to do with the show. That was their choice."

The Soul Train Gang was a quintet consisting of Gerald Brown, Terry Brown, Patricia Williamson, Judy Jones, and Hollis Pippin, and their first album would be *Don Cornelius Presents the Soul Train Gang*. Produced by Griffey and Cornelius, the collection's most memorable track was "Soul Train '75," which became the show's new theme. With Williamson replaced by Denise Smith and MFSB guitarist Norman Harris handling production, a second LP was primarily recorded at Philadelphia's hit-making Sigma Sound. But except for "Soul Train Theme '76 (Get on Board)," which would replace "Soul Train '75," the album made no waves. That had to have been embarrassing for all involved.

Daniel had a brief stint with the Soul Train Gang when Pippin left the group during a promotional tour. With his showmanship and popularity on the show, Daniel shined during the tour. Back in Los Angeles, he was rehearsing with Watley at her house when Cornelius called and asked to speak to him. Don told Daniel that the Soul Train Gang was " 'over. It's finished. I have a new project I want you to do,' " Daniel recalled. "He asked me immediately, 'Do you know a girl who can sing?' " Daniel wasn't sure how good a singer Watley was. Her mother, Rose, sang in the church choir, but he really hadn't heard his dance partner croon. Initially he called Grand Rapids, reaching out to a cousin of the DeBarge singing clan, but the young lady was pregnant. So together he and Watley practiced vocals, singing along to records by favorites Barbra Streisand and Diana Ross.

While Daniel and Watley were practicing, a producer named Simon Soussan created a track called "Uptown Festival," a disco-flavored medley of classic Motown hits. Two studio singers, Gary Mumford and Cleo Kennedy, sang on the record. Coincidentally, Kennedy was a singer in the same choir as Watley's mother. The principals of Soul Train Records purchased the track, feeling it was a commercial record they could use to rebrand the label with another act. It's not clear who came up with the name Shalamar, but that's what they called the group. Though not a huge hit, "Uptown Festival" made a mark, reaching No. 22 on the R&B chart and making some noise in the United Kingdom.

They kept Mumford, who was a vocal teacher in the Bay Area, and added Daniel and Watley to fill out the trio. "Jeffrey and I were chosen to be in Shalamar because we were the most popular dancers on the show," Watley said. "We had been in magazines . . . It was another dream come true for me, because singing was always what I wanted to do. Funny thing was they assumed I couldn't sing, though. Once we came off this promotional tour promoting 'Uptown Festival' and it was time to record the album, there was talk that they were going to get another girl. You know I'm hearing rumors. I'm going, 'You don't need another girl. I can sing.'"

So she auditioned by singing Streisand's "Evergreen," and that sealed the deal. Watley can be heard on most of the seven tracks on 1977's "Uptown Festival" album, which included a couple of straightforward covers of Motown classics ("Ooo Baby Baby," "Forever Came Today") and one song penned by Don Cornelius ("High on Life").

When it was time to record Shalamar's second album, *Disco Gardens*, Mumford was no longer in the group, replaced by Gerald Brown, who'd been the original lead singer of the Soul Train Gang. But there were bigger changes occurring around the group. At some point between 1977 and 1978, the Cornelius-Griffey recording partnership was dissolved and the surviving label was renamed SOLAR (Sound of Los Angeles) Records.

Both men were publicly vague on why they split, but there was no obvious acrimony. *Soul Train* would, in fact, loyally promote SOLAR acts during the label's incredibly successful run from its founding in 1978 into the late 1980s. Much like the mistake Cornelius made by not keeping the *Soul Train* name on the "TSOP" track, he was ending his partnership with Griffey just as he was on the verge of becoming the most successful R&B mogul of the early 1980s. Chuck Johnson, who'd work at *Soul Train* for more than a decade and would later join SOLAR Records, gives some insight into the differences between Cornelius and Griffey.

"As a marketing man, Don was always ahead of his time," Johnson said. "He had an eye for talent and great vision. Don was tightly wrapped and controlling, but Dick was very outgoing and open to trying any idea and take a risk." People say that opposites attract in love, but in business opposites can sometimes irritate the hell out of each other. Perhaps, over time, the two men's contrasting personalities and desire to be in charge pushed them apart. Cornelius would reign successfully over his *Soul Train* fiefdom for decades, while Griffey would go on to build a formidable musical empire.

The roots of SOLAR's ascendance could be found in the production and songwriting credits of *Disco Gardens*. Three of the seven songs on the album were written or cowritten by Leon Sylvers III; he also produced the entire album. To most folks, the twenty-four-year-old was just one of the older members of the family group the Sylvers, who'd been recording since 1971 on the heels of the Jackson Five's success. But as early as 1973, when Leon was just twenty, he was already composing songs for his siblings and building a reputation in music-business circles as a promising hit maker. Griffey recruited Sylvers heavily, convincing him to leave his family group and become SOLAR's in-house producer. A deft bassist as well as a talented songwriter, Sylvers would cowrite the vibrant "Take That to the Bank," the percolating dance track that established the dynamic, propulsive sound that would become the label's trademark. Watley's voice was well showcased by Sylvers, setting an approach that would become a signature of the Shalamar sound.

The song wasn't a huge hit, but it gave Shalamar and SOLAR a trademark sound and made Watley a genuine recording artist. But her start wasn't as glamorous as she'd have liked. "It wasn't a fairy tale," she said. "It was a lot of hard work. It was before music videos, pretty much, so we toured all the time and not in the best conditions. Terrible bus with no heat in the winter. No bunk beds—just seats. Sometimes I would feel like I was in a fifties movie where you see the artists schlepping their equipment and they're on the bus. A learning experience."

Watley didn't feel she received the warmest reception during Shalamar's first performance on *Soul Train*.

Watley: Probably a few months before, we had still been on the show and on the *Soul Train* line. "Why did they pick her and why did they pick him" was the kind of vibe [I] felt. There was kind of a bitter intensity, because a lot of those same dancers were there, and they were giving the evil eye . . . I appreciated it, but I didn't really savor it, because it was a lot of negative energy at that time. It wasn't until I went back later on my own that I could really let it sink in. Again, it was being in a survival-of-the-fittest mode the first time I did it.

Daniel, who would regularly stop by tapings even after Shalamar had hit records, often felt in the middle of a gentle tug-of-war between Don and Griffey.

Daniel: I'm a dancer, and I've always been a dancer, and so when Shalamar is not on the road, I would sneak back into *Soul Train*, and Don would egg me on. "You know Dick Griffey doesn't want you to dance here. You better not dance." What? He knew he was using reverse psychology. Then Dick Griffey would watch it. "Jeffrey, I see you dancing down there on *Soul Train*. You're a star now. You don't need to be dancing on no TV show." So I was caught between Don and Dick, and it was hard because both were like my fathers.

Well, if Watley had haters and Daniel was torn, the band's third popular album surely eased any tension. With Howard Hewett, a smooth crooner with a silky tenor handling lead vocals, Shalamar's *Big Fun* would begin a four-year run of danceable hits for the trio.

Other regular *Soul Train* performers (the Whispers, Lakeside, Carrie Lucas) would populate the SOLAR Records lineup in its early years. It makes you wonder what would have happened if Don had stayed in the record business.

While he never had another label, Don did manage another act, one that got tremendous exposure on *Soul Train* but never sold many records. O'Bryan McCoy Burnette II, professionally known as O'Bryan, was born in North Carolina, where he began playing piano at six years old and then performing at talent shows. His family moved to Santa Ana, California, in 1974, where he became active in his local Baptist church. He had a sweet voice with a high-pitched falsetto that was noticed by Melanee Kersey, the wife of Ron "Have Mercy" Kersey, once a fixture in the vibrant Philadelphia music scene, who'd moved to the West Coast.

Kersey, who'd been part of the disco band the Trammps, initially recruited O'Bryan to be part of a vocal group. When that deal fell through, Kersey introduced O'Bryan to Don, who was impressed. Together the two music vets formed Friendship Productions and successfully shopped O'Bryan to Capitol Records in the early 1980s.

Marketed with a Jheri curl, eyeliner, shirts with the top three buttons open, and occasionally a red leather jacket—all echoes of Michael Jackson—O'Bryan would release four albums between 1982 and 1986 and have nine charting singles including "The Gigolo," which went to No. 5 on the R&B singles chart. Don certainly supported him, having his artist on *Soul Train* numerous times during his recording career.

Despite this prime exposure, the singer never earned a gold single or album, and after he was dropped by Capitol, O'Bryan didn't make another record until 2007. His only truly memorable contribution to *Soul Train* lore was recording "*Soul Train*'s A-Comin'," which became the show's theme in 1983. So while *Soul Train* was absolutely a great platform for black talent, regular exposure did not guarantee record sales or genuine celebrity.

One more note on Don's adventures in recording: Cheryl Song says that Don tried to put together another Shalamar-styled group, using a singer and some of the *Soul Train* dancers. A vocalist named Terry Stanton would have been the front man, with two of the most charismatic dancers to ever appear on *Soul Train*—Song and the fiery New Yorker Rosie Perez—adding multiculti showmanship. "I thought this was it!" Song said. "This was my one chance to be a serious artist . . . We met a couple of times with Don, and we met with a record company." But this multicultural dream group never happened.

Chapter 11
1980s

||||||||||||||||||||||||||||||||||||||

IN THE early 1980s, Don Cornelius began having migraine head-aches. When he finally went in for tests, the TV producer was diag-nosed with a congenital malformation of the blood vessels in his brain. On November 12, 1982, he underwent a twenty-one-hour operation to save his life. Despite the near-death experience, Don quipped after the surgery that "you choose your brain surgeons for their stamina." The procedure would have long-term repercussions. In the years to come, Don would say he was never "what I used to be as a manager or an entrepreneur" due to the lingering effects of that operation. Nevertheless, a determined Don was back to work on the *Soul Train* set just six months after the operation.

As personally challenging as this recovery had to have been for Don, outwardly he didn't appear slowed down to either the young people who danced on the show or his music-industry peers. *Soul Train*, along with the music industry, would go through profound changes in the new decade, much of it driven by technology that would alter the kinds of acts who'd appear on the show and what they'd look and sound like. Moreover, the competition for the eyeballs of music fans would escalate in ways *Soul Train* could not compete with.

The sound of R&B would evolve from the raw funk and elegant disco associated with *Soul Train*'s early years to records driven by drum machines and keyboard-created bass and horn lines. Bands would shrink from nine- and ten-piece aggregations to two- and three-member groups and, in a few special cases, influential one-man bands. In the most unlikely development, soul singing, which had been the pride and joy of black artistic expression since the early sixties, would be challenged as the chief vehicle for black self-expression by a generation of nonsingers from New York. In addition, the turntable, devised as a tool for playing music, would become an instrument in itself.

And just as technology would alter the sound of music, new ways to consume it would present new competition for Don's enterprise.

THE MUSIC video channel MTV premiered in August 1981, but it didn't really have an immediate effect on *Soul Train*. In its early years, MTV failed to include R&B artists in its regular playlist, sticking to the kind of rock-centric programming philosophy that had created musical apartheid on American radio, where it had been very difficult (and sometimes impossible) for black performers to get programmed on many of the nation's biggest radio stations. Network executives said they were utilizing the then-popular album-oriented rock (AOR) format to decide who did and didn't appear on MTV. If they'd been true to that, maybe few would have protested.

But when white artists who played in an R&B or "black" style—such as Culture Club and Hall & Oates—were put in MTV rotation and black R&B artists were not, it was clear MTV's decisions had more to do with skin color than sound. Moreover, MTV was breaking bands with good videos but no durability, while gifted, charismatic musicians like Rick James, whose music did fit the format, found it hard to get on the network's play list and aggressively protested that exclusion.

Even after MTV embraced Michael Jackson's "Billie Jean" video in 1983 and began allowing a few other black crossover performers, such as Prince and Whitney Houston, on its airwaves, there was still a bounty of great black acts and musicians who were denied the exposure to millions of potential young buyers because MTV wouldn't touch them. One legitimate explanation the MTV programmers had was that the few videos that were made for black acts were often of poor quality. But if MTV wouldn't play them, why would record labels finance a $125,000 video? During the early to mid-1980s, the average budget for most black performers' music videos was about $35,000, which kept the production quality poor and the ambition low in comparison to videos for white artists.

To satisfy the appetite for visual representations of black music, a number of ventures were announced after MTV's launch. In 1982 Inner City Broadcasting, a black-owned company that controlled a number of major-market radio stations including New York's WBLS-FM and Los Angeles's KUTE-FM, announced its Apollo Entertainment Network, which had a goal of providing forty-two hours of programming to 250 cable systems. In March of that year, a weekly syndicated video show called *R&B Express* started airing in 420 markets. A ninety-minute music-video-based special called *Sultans of Soul*, hosted by sitcom star Tim Reid (*WKRP in Cincinnati*) aired with an eye toward becoming a half-hour show. Don Kirshner Productions, the folks behind NBC's popular *The Midnight Special* concert series, produced a two-hour special called *Rhythm 'n' Rolls*. A group called Bronze Star Productions was producing a weekly video show named *Jammin' on the Tube*.

Most of these endeavors either never aired or survived only a year or more. The one enterprise from this era that took hold was Black

Entertainment Television (BET). Owned by black businessman Robert Johnson along with his deep-pocketed backer, media mogul John Malone, BET started slowly in August 1981 and was available to only two million households by 1984. The programming during its early years primarily comprised old 1970s sitcoms, movies featuring black actors, faith-based broadcasts, and infomercials. There was little original programming, and music wasn't yet a huge part of their mix.

In a long *Billboard* magazine piece titled "As Programming Demands Rise, Black Music Increasingly Visible" that ran on June 5, 1982, BET merited only a single sentence: "The Black Entertainment Television network is extending its programming service this summer with a major portion of time devoted to music." As more black videos became available, Johnson soon recognized that they could be a huge source of free programming on which he could build his network. Record labels and artists, fed up with getting the cold shoulder from MTV, began to support BET and traveled down to its Washington, DC, studios to do interviews and to tape (mostly lip-synched) performances. It was clear that once BET began airing music videos pretty much exclusively, it would eventually have an impact on *Soul Train*'s weekly broadcast, but no one knew to what degree.

This challenge to *Soul Train*'s supremacy in broadcasting black music would, however, occur only incrementally, due to BET's many challenges in becoming available on key urban markets' cable systems. In fact, it would be ten years after its launch before BET could truly claim that it was available nationwide.

Black neighborhoods, even in major markets like New York and in crucial southern cities, were often the last to gain cable access. If you lived in midtown Manhattan, you could watch MTV but not be able to see BET in Harlem, much less in black outer-borough hoods like Bedford-Stuyvesant and Crown Heights. When cable was finally available, many working-class and poor households often had to decide whether it was worth the additional monthly bill (which inspired a lively illegal business in bootleg cable boxes). Local cable operators had to be convinced that BET belonged on their schedules. The 1980s amounted to an arduous climb for the cable start-up.

Unfortunately, Cornelius and Johnson, both pioneers in the business of visual black entertainment, would never have much of a personal relationship. Their business models were so different that neither felt the need to cultivate the other. Plus both men had such healthy egos it's hard to imagine either feeling vulnerable enough to open up to the other. But this doesn't mean *Soul Train* and BET wouldn't do any business together in the 1980s and 1990s. It just meant the founders of these two kindred black institutions didn't necessarily see the value of a close business relationship, and they acted accordingly.

Meanwhile, in the wider world of American media there was much to be excited about vis-à-vis the black image. In September 1980, Eddie Murphy joined the cast of NBC's *Saturday Night Live*, becoming an instant pop star with his chameleonlike impressions, pop-culture references, and youthful exuberance. He'd quickly make the transition to movies (*48 Hours, Beverly Hills Cop*) and become Hollywood's biggest black star since Sidney Poitier in the 1960s. Longtime sports announcer Bryant Gumbel debuted as coanchor of the *Today* show in 1982, putting an energetic black presence on the nation's number one morning show. Oprah Winfrey began her incredible run of success when she was named cohost of *AM Chicago* in 1984, which would be the launching pad for an unprecedented media empire. Even before the premiere of *The Cosby Show* in September 1984, comedian Bill Cosby was already the leading commercial spokesperson in America, having successfully hawked everything from banks to Jell-O prior to his hit TV sitcom. He'd go on to rival President Ronald Reagan as 1980s America's favorite surrogate father.

In music, black recording superstars would emerge of a magnitude unimaginable when Don Cornelius started broadcasting from a small Chicago studio in 1969. My first interview as *Record World*'s black music editor in January 1981 was with one of these future superstars—a young man known as Prince—prior to the release of his landmark third album, *Dirty Mind*, a record that was a harbinger of the future, full of tracks with new-wave rock flavor and sexually explicit lyrics (referencing orgies and incest) sung in a high-pitched voice in the R&B love-man tradition but with rock 'n' roll abandon. Musically, it would be hugely influential because of its innovative use of keyboards, drum machines, and vocal arrangements; its lyrics expressed a sexual frankness that would embolden and anticipate a new direction in songwriting (which, during our interview, Prince called his "real reality") that would titillate his generation and alienate many old heads, including Cornelius.

Prince's record pushed the boundaries of black music while maintaining connections to its traditions. It was a balancing act he would maintain throughout his brilliant career. Born and raised in Minneapolis, Minnesota, a city with a small black population, Prince was always very conscious of leaping over the barriers that constrained most artists of color. The buzzword for Prince, as well as for Michael Jackson, Whitney Houston, Lionel Richie, Quincy Jones, Tina Turner, and many others was *crossover*, a strategy for growing your music-buying audience from a black audience to a larger white one. It was the obsession of the major record labels, since their goal was not just to go platinum (one million or so records, most likely at first to black audiences) but multiplatinum, which usually meant reaching regular white record buyers and, eventually, casual fans who only purchased recordings by big, mainstream pop stars.

Which is probably why Prince would never perform on *Soul Train* during his commercial peak in the eighties. It wasn't until the 1993–94 season, after he was fading as a record seller and his Artist Formerly Known as Prince phase, that he appeared on the broadcast. *Soul Train* did run a video by Prince on episode #416 in the 1982–83 season, and acts he produced, such as the Time (episode #375, 1981–82) and Vanity 6 (episode #410, 1982–83), graced Don's stage. But one of the premier blacks stars of the eighties never was on the show, something unthinkable a decade earlier.

It's worth noting that Lionel Richie, who'd appeared on *Soul Train* regularly as a member of the Commodores, never performed on the show during his long run of solo hits, and Whitney Houston, the dominant female vocalist of the era, appeared only once (episode #476, in the 1984–85 season) to promote her record-setting debut album. Once the diva broke pop, Houston never came back. No one was more aware of these omissions and what they meant, both for his show and for the black music business in general, than Don.

In 1982, I moved from *Record World* magazine to the industry's number one trade publication, *Billboard*, where I would cover black music through 1989. On April 6, 1985, I wrote a column that addressed the vexing question of crossover that featured comments from *Soul Train*'s founder. The column was titled "Don Cornelius Speaks Out on the Crossover Issue" and was sparked by Los Angeles R&B radio station KACE's boycott of all records released by Warner Bros. artists after the label failed to put as many promotional dollars into black radio as it had pop radio to support a Prince show at the Forum. KACE's management cited this as an example of how crossover by a black star could have a negative economic effect on black businesses.

In response to this, Cornelius sent an open letter to eleven major black radio program directors. He had no problem with any individual act or label, but wrote "to express my concern over the ever developing 'he's (she's) not black' syndrome in referring to black crossover artists . . . For record companies, this unfortunate approach is a rather insidious form of pragmatism in that it is widely used to deter lesser known black artists and managers from requesting the services being provided to crossover artists. In being denied the full services they see preferred artists receive, the artist and his representative are simply told, 'But he's not black.' Not what you'd call the fairest way to compare one artist to another.

"In my view, the most damaging effect by far is seen in the attitudes of the artists who are being told they are 'not black.' Their response, almost without exception, has been a de-emphasis of the importance of black radio, black attendance at concerts, and embarrassingly I admit, *Soul Train* appearances."

Later in the letter Don wrote, "The original intent of the 'he's (she's) not black' syndrome may very well have been the removal of distinctions by color which I believe everyone, including myself, would welcome. If indeed this is our goal, I say our goal has been perverted somewhere along the line, for that clearly is what is taking place. Those of us who labor in this industry are all naturally very proud whenever an artist crosses over, since we were usually there in the beginning. The problem we're facing now is something akin to amnesia. It is my hope that eventually black crossover artists come to understand that as important as pop exposure may be, it is not necessary to avoid communication or contact with the black audience or media to hold on to it."

While Don's words were strong, reflecting the concerns of so many involved with black music at the time, some in the business felt that Don was being a bit hypocritical, since *Soul Train* itself had employed its own "crossover" strategy from 1983 to 1985. These years were probably the most polarizing in *Soul Train*'s history as Don and the show's production team struggled to adapt (and attempted to co-opt) the music-video-driven energy generated by MTV. Music videos were made part of the programming mix and white artists, most not soulful or connected to black traditions, found their way onto the *Soul Train* stage.

Some longtime fans of the show speculate that during his recovery from brain surgery, Don decided to revamp the show. Whether the changes occurred as fallout from his surgery or not, Don clearly rethought *Soul Train*'s mission during the 1983–85 period. The MTV-ization of *Soul Train* went so far that at some point he even stopped the "love, peace, and *soul*" sign-off. For hard-core soul music fans, with the introduction of videos and so many white fans, the new show was difficult to take. Meanwhile, younger white pop viewers, many of whose localities were not yet wired for cable, were now attracted to the show. It was a calculated trade-off that started with episode #438 in the middle of the 1983–84 season and ran to episode #506 near the end of 1985–86. Twenty-one white performers appeared on the show either in cameos, videos, or studio performances during that stretch. That's the highest number for any period in *Soul Train* history. Some of these bookings made perfect sense: Teena Marie, Culture Club, Hall & Oates, the Tom Tom Club, and Sheena Easton either made overtly R&B music or compatible dance music. All of them also had a strong cultural identification with black culture, either because they'd been played regularly on black radio, had expressed their admiration for it in song or interviews, or had been "sponsored" by a black star (for instance, Easton had been produced by Prince).

Ex-Eagle (and county-rock icon) Don Henley, soap opera heart-throb Jack Wagner, and Weird Al (represented by his "Eat It" video) were curious enough bookings, but someone on the programming team had a real weakness for new-wave bands. The Romantics, Spandau Ballet, Howard Jones, Berlin, A-ha, the Thompson Twins, Animotion: even if you decide to give *Soul Train*'s bookers the ben-efit of the doubt with the Pet Shop Boys, that's still a lineup more appropriate for a show hosted by Downtown Julie Brown than Don Cornelius.

While Duran Duran would appear on episode #531 in the 1986–87 season and ABC on episode #553 in 1987–88, *Soul Train*'s new-wave fetish ended as quickly as it appeared. While a lot of viewers had problems with these bookings, some considering it a betrayal of *Soul*

Train's commitment to black culture, the Roots' Amir Thompson argues that it opened up black viewers to a universe of music they'd have otherwise ignored.

Thompson: You know, I know there was a lot of controversy over the sort of pop period of *Soul Train*. But I didn't know who the Police were. I saw them on *Soul Train*. That was one of the most controversial things. It was, like, on the Teena Marie episode of 1984. "And now for a video—here's the Police and 'Wrapped Around Your Finger.'" Everyone in the house is like, What the hell? The Police on *Soul Train*. Great. That was my first introduction to a lot of things I didn't get to see. Without that, I don't think I would be as obsessed with music as I am, or as immersed in music as I am.

DANCER PROFILE: Louie "Ski" Carr

Louie "Ski" Carr had the slang, the style, and the steps to make him a significant fixture on the show in the 1980s. Like earlier *Soul Train* dancer stars, being on the show led him to a long career as a choreographer and style muse. Raised in Inglewood, California, not far from the Great Western Forum, home of the Los Angeles Lakers, Carr was a six-foot-five-inch Blaxican, or black Mexican, teen who spent a lot of his time on the local basketball courts at Rogers Park. Ballin' one afternoon in the 1980s, Carr ran into a group of young men who called themselves Cuttys. Since this was LA in the 1980s, you'd expect the Cuttys to be gang, but unlike the Bloods or Crips, they were a social group, not a criminal enterprise. "Cuttys," Carr said, "means like brothers that stick together. They made me a Cutty, and I took that and just made it a whole Cutty vibe experience."

For Carr, this identification with the Cutty mack ethos defined his life. "Everything is Cutty mack," he said. "If you see one of your other Cuttys over there, and it's crowded, and he can't hear you, you just throw the Cutty finger, and he knows you're there. All our dances had names. There was the go dida. You had the Cutty finger. You had the ski slide. Everything was named. Everything had a movement."

Cuttys were flamboyant dressers, and Carr was well-known for his hats, glasses (actual glass optional), and a variety of flashy, flowing suits. The dancers Carr admired had a strong fashion sense: Elvis Presley, James Brown, and Michael Jackson. Some of Jackson's signature moves, such as pointing at his socks, were incorporated into Carr's dancing.

Carr was a *Soul Train* fan and, using the access of his friend

George Chambers's girlfriend, a dancer on the show, Carr schemed to gain entry. "I used to say, 'Hey, George, you got to get your girl on there. I got to get on the *Train*. I'll do anything, you know, to get on that show.' So she took me on. I had to make a first impression, so I went and bought a black tux." Sadly, that tux was no magic ticket. Carr was turned down the first and second times he tried to get into a Saturday taping. "I'm saying to myself, I'm dressed, I got a tux on, you know, what's wrong?" On his third attempt, Carr was finally granted entry. "As soon as I went in, I went straight to the stage because there's like a riser that the good dancers get to dance on, and I figured I'm six five, I'm gonna dance right there and make it seem like I'm onstage with them."

> **Carr:** So I'm doing all that, my crazy antics—sticking my finger up like I'm on top of the stage, et cetera. I see Don talking to the same guy that let me in, whispering something, and [he] pointed over there to me. I think, "Oh, I'm in trouble now. I'm about to be kicked out or something." Boom. After the song he comes to me says, "Don wants you to dance on top of the riser like the other dancers." So for me that was a start, and now I'm up there with the girl with the long hair. I'm up there doing my thing. They position you up there with a partner. The partner kind of got mad because I never stayed. I always had to keep moving and doing my Elvis moves, James Brown moves, and my whole style.

Carr's stature and style made him an immediate viewer favorite. "I have this, you know, certain Cutty mack style," said Carr, "which is just doing whatever you can to the music, however it moves you. If it's whispering in the girl's ear—I'm really whispering. When the camera comes by, tell me so I could be ready with the move. Here comes the camera: boom,

I'm pointing and nobody's even over there. I was, like, never formally trained in dance, but I think just that style."

New Edition, a quintet of vocalists from Boston, brought a hip-hop energy to the traditional black vocal group, mixing street dance moves with old-fashioned vocal choreography. For folks being raised on hip-hop's emerging aesthetics in the early 1980s, Bobby Brown, Michael Bivins, Ricky DeVoe, Ralph Tresvant, and Ronnie Bell were the new Temptations. But to the quintet's members, Carr was the real star. When the group made their first *Soul Train* appearance (episode #451, at the start of the 1983–84 season), they were the ones looking for an introduction.

> **Carr:** This girl says these young cats, New Edition from Boston, want to meet you. I was like, Cool. I'm sitting with my Cutty macks. They roll with me. New Edition are all sitting in their chairs looking at me . . . They was like, "Man, we like your style. How you do all your things and, like, you jumping from one stage to the next like you was, like, skiing? So, you know, we want you to be onstage with us. We're going to sing this song, 'Candy Girl.' Please just come on do your thing, point to your socks, do it with the finger and the shouting and the kicks." I was like, "Okay, look, don't tell Don, because Don will not give it a go. Let's just do it. I got you. Don't worry about it."

"Candy Girl," like much of New Edition's first album, was a Jackson Five–influenced record that echoed the black pop past while feeling very contemporary. About midway through the song, Bobby Brown motioned with a Cutty finger, and Carr jumped on stage.

> **Carr:** I go to touch the *Soul Train* logo. Come in between them, throw a Mike kick, point to the argyles. They all point to the argyles. I'm still in that moment, but I'm still thinking nobody got permis-

sion from Don. I hope I don't get kicked off. First thing he says to New Edition is, "Big Lou, stay offstage with the singers." But then he says facetiously, "You guys asked him, you like him?" They was like, "Yeah, we like his style." And Don was like, "He can't pop or lock," which means I can't dance. They was like, "Yeah, but he can George, though." Somebody told them my name was George, and I used to wear suits. You know, the whole *Gentlemen's Quarterly* style with the suits, ties, shoes, the Gators, Stacy Adams too. And so when they would buy suits they would call them George, after me.

That first onstage collaboration began an enduring friendship between Carr and the various members of New Edition, a band that would form and re-form many times over the years. When three members split off to form the trio Bell Biv DeVoe, Carr was part of their team, appearing at shows and in videos, including a memorable night at the Forum. "There's footage of me and Bel Biv DeVoe onstage at the Forum where the Lakers won the championship in the eighties," he recalled fondly. "[Laker guard] Norm Nixon's right there with two Honey Dips and Debbie Allen [his future wife]. Magic Johnson's over here dancing. He's looking at me and giving the Cutty finger."

Even with all of his non–*Soul Train* notoriety, Carr is still best remembered for his jaunts down the *Soul Train* line. "I would just come up with these most ridiculous skits and scenes in my mind, like movie things," he said. "I remember one time I came down and my boy Tom Tom pretending like he was talking and kissing my girl. Then I come on stage, and I come with a gun and I shoot him with a fake gun, and he falls. My boy TV comes out with stun guns. Now we going down the line shooting people and stun-gunning people, right? After that, Don says, 'Ski, don't be pulling guns out on the *Soul Train* line. Come on.' I was like, 'It was a fake gun,' and Don's like, 'I know, but it's a family show.'"

Chapter 12

HIP-HOP VS. *SOUL TRAIN*

IN THE SPRING OF 1980 Curtis Walker—also known as Kurtis Blow, Harlem native, City College of New York attendee, and all of nineteen years old—stepped onto the *Soul Train* set for episode #336 and became the first hip-hop figure to appear on the show. The headliner was the self-contained band L.T.D., featuring deep-voiced vocalist Jeffrey Osborne, but Blow's appearance was the highlight of the taping. Overjoyed to be on the show, the young MC performed "The Breaks" live to a track for an excited group of dancers. Then Don Cornelius walked on stage to do the customary interview. For Blow, this was to be the high point of an extraordinary day. He'd flown in that morning from New York on his first trip to the City of Angels. On the heels of his first single, "Christmas Rappin'," and the gold "The Breaks," Blow had already performed in Amsterdam, London, and Paris.

But for a ghetto kid from Harlem, being on *Soul Train* was a new pinnacle. Moreover, Blow had started his career in hip-hop as a break-dancer and had idolized Don Campbell and the Lockers. Blow had checked into his hotel that morning and then sped over to the *Soul Train* set, geeking out that his dressing room was right next to *Fame* star Irene Cara's.

Don had been cordial when greeting Blow backstage and gave in when the rapper requested that he be allowed to perform live to track, rather than lip-synch "The Breaks," since (a) he'd never lip-synched in his young career and (b) he needed the crowd interplay that was essential to hip-hop. When Cornelius walked on the stage, Blow expected the standard *Soul Train* treatment. "We know *Soul Train*, after the performances, and you're standing onstage, and Don Cornelius comes out. He gives a couple of accolades: 'How about another round of applause for this great artist.' I've seen this all my life. I'm anticipating this, and I'm ready for this . . . So he comes out, you know he has the microphone, he comes up and stands next to me, and he says, 'I don't really know what everyone is making so much fuss about all this hip-hop, but nonetheless you heard him here, Mr. Kurtis Blow."

The MC recalled that moment with sad clarity. "I was heartbroken. My heart actually left and traveled south to my feet, and I was stunned and shocked. And I don't know what I said. I don't think I said anything. I don't know what I said, but whatever it was, believe me . . . It's not really what I wanted to say."

Don's ambivalence toward hip-hop was shared by most of the black music gatekeepers of his generation, be they major-label executives, radio programmers, or R&B musicians. Hip-hop seemed to challenge the essentials of black music: the stars didn't sing, a DJ playing records served as the band, and "songs" weren't structured in the verse-verse-chorus-verse-bridge-verse structure of standard pop songs. Moreover, the mainstream black popular music that Cornelius—and everyone in the black music biz—was heavily invested in had been trending toward an upscale, clean-sounding, self-conscious sophistication that was reflected in clothing as well as sound. Male artists were wearing lots of eyeliner and sporting jelled hair (either Jheri curl or California curls, depending on the product's purveyor). It was a very LA look, one the dancers on *Soul Train* proudly displayed.

The stripped-down (but no less codified) look coming out of New York's hip-hop scene represented a contrast to (or perhaps an attack on) the black mainstream and the assumptions about acceptable black maleness behind them. It wasn't simply a generation gap that separated Don from rap—though clearly that was part of it—but a disagreement about how to be "black." In the 1970s *Soul Train* had promoted a liberated funkiness that took cutting-edge style into homes across the country. But from the time Blow took the *Soul Train* onward, Cornelius's soulful train would be running a little behind the sonic vehicles transporting hip-hop.

Years later, Cornelius talked about *Soul Train*'s sometimes uneasy relationship with this new musical movement.

Cornelius: Hip-hop kind of took *Soul Train* by surprise because we thought it was something that might not stick, and we didn't jump in with both feet. But apparently we had to put both feet in the pot, because young people became so committed to hip-hop, and it became the culture it is today. People look at you funny if you act like you don't know what it is. The younger demographics will simply turn away from you because you're making it clear to them that you don't know what you're doing. What's made it beautiful in an overall sense, and why no other genre has accomplished what it has, is that hip-hop/rap are so inclusive. It's inclusive in the sense that you don't have to be Quincy Jones to succeed in hip-hop. There are people who have carved successful careers in the hip-hop/rap media who, thirty years ago, would not have been able to participate in the music biz. It's part of the black culture, and if you learn to understand it, you can actually make a good living out of it.

With this pragmatic view as Don's guide, rap artists would slowly become part of the *Soul Train* mix. The first performers with a huge rap hit were the Sugar Hill Gang, a trio of inexperienced MCs from the New York–New Jersey area cobbled together by Sugar Hill Records co-owner Sylvia Robinson (a former R&B crooner who'd appeared on *Soul Train* in 1973 with the erotic hit "Pillow Talk"). Robinson and the three MCs put together "Rapper's Delight," a Top Ten hit all over the globe and a massive hit in the United States. Although this landmark recording was released in 1979, the Sugar Hill Gang didn't appear on *Soul Train* until a year after its debut. I believe one reason Blow was booked on the show before the Sugar Hill Gang is that he was signed to Mercury Records, a major label with a strong, ongoing relationship with Cornelius—who needed the label's cooperation if he wanted to book its more mainstream R&B acts. Sugar Hill Records, born out of the ruins of R&B All Platinum Records, out of Englewood, New Jersey, was an independent label with no such leverage.

"I guess he was hesitant with bringing [hip-hop] on," recalled Sugar Hill Gang member Big Bank Hank. "But you can't stop a hit . . . If you can't stop it, you might as well get out of the way, because here it comes. It was like you were riding the perfect wave."

A reflection of Sugar Hill's absence of clout was that neither the group's three members nor its management were able to persuade Cornelius to drop his lip-synch policy. Where Blow was able to perform live, the trio was forced to lip-synch its performance. "Hip-hop is about being able to flow and rhythmically go in and out of the music and change it whenever you want to. Now you're stuck because you have to go with what the track is. You can't play with the music." Still, the performance went well. "Oh, they lost their mind," Hank recalled. "They just loved it."

As the eighties unfolded and rap began its long progression from New York underground culture to mainstream brand machine, *Soul*

Train would showcase top MCs overwhelmingly from New York and elsewhere on the East Coast: everyone from Run-D.M.C. to LL Cool J to Whodini to the Beastie Boys. But several of the artists felt a chill from Cornelius and some of the *Soul Train* staffers. Members of Run-D.M.C. would, incredibly, tell reporters that they felt more welcome at their initial visit to *American Bandstand* than they did on *Soul Train*.

Ahmir Thompson, an ardent *Soul Train* viewer and future hip-hop icon himself, remembers these appearances well. "I'm glad that it was included, but I more or less felt that maybe it was tokenism. Maybe it's kind of hard to see change." He felt that a lot of the tone of Cornelius's interaction with rappers during the 1980s was "stand-offish" and along the lines of "How long do you think this is gonna last?" Thompson knew this attitude well, since "that's how my father was: 'That's not music.' He would always cover his ears. I'm glad it was included because, again, my first view of the Sugar Hill Gang or Grandmaster Flash and the Furious Five was on *Soul Train* . . . I could tell that Don was a little uncomfortable in embracing it, but as a businessman, I'm glad he was smart enough to give in."

If Cornelius tolerated the New York MCs for whom boasting about their rhyme skills was the essential topic, he was actively hostile toward the crack-era narratives that gained popularity around 1989 and, ironically, came out of some of the same South Central Los Angeles communities (Compton, Long Beach, Inglewood) as the majority of his dancers. Led by Ice-T, N.W.A, Snoop Doggy Dogg, Warren G, and Tupac Shakur and built primarily on samples from funk bands, this genre became a cultural-commercial phenomenon that initially didn't need radio play to sell records, but by 1994 it found its obscenity-free singles and party-hardy videos landing in heavy rotation—not just on black radio and BET, but on MTV as well.

Moreover, the charisma of the star gangsta rappers, plus the tabloid violence of the crack era, led many of them to star in Hollywood features (*New Jack City*, *Boyz N the Hood*, *Menace II Society*, *Trespass*,

Juice) that generated platinum-selling soundtracks. By 1994 the ubiquity of these performers, as well as their drug-referenced, blood-splattered, sexually raw (and often sexist) records, outraged many.

Spurred by activist C. Delores Tucker and other elders in the black community, on February 11, 1994, the Subcommittee on Commerce, Consumer Protection, and Competitiveness of the Committee on Energy and Commerce in the House of Representatives held the first of two hearings on whether there should be a ratings system for recorded music. While lip service was given to sexism and violence in rock, hip-hop was the clear target of the hearings. I was there that day to give historical context on the music and to support free speech in music.

Don Cornelius was there, too. We spoke briefly at the hearings, but it was a strained conversation because he was there to attack gangsta rap and support a mandatory ratings system for all music. I'm reprinting Cornelius's testimony in full because I think it perfectly captures the ambivalence of the R&B establishment's feelings about hip-hop in general and gangsta rap in particular during the nineties.

In order to understand the ever-growing popularity of the music form known as Gangsta Rap, it is necessary to briefly explore rap music in general and some of the reasons why rap has become the musical entertainment preference of many millions of youth and young adults throughout the free world. Originally intended as a purely entertaining form of street and night club or dance club rhyming or poetry spoken over prerecorded music tracks, rap music has evolved into a legitimate, popular music art form through which many young musicians, publicists and recorded music producers who are connected, often sociologically to America's underclass (particularly that segment which is African-American), are able to express various kinds of commentary on some of the harder realities of life as it exists in many of America's African-American ghettos.

The preponderance of recorded rap music which deals with ghetto life is likely to include extremely profane lyrics which tend to glorify violence or illegal firearms or drug use. The lyrics which are degrading or disrespectful to women, or sexually explicit lyrics. This kind of rap has become widely known as "hard core" rap. Rap artists who specialize in hard core are well aware going in that hard core records, for obvious reasons, get no radio station airplay whatsoever, which would literally be the kiss of death for any other recording artist. This is usually not the fate, however, in the case of hard core rappers, thanks to what is known as the "underground" retailing market, a random array of small, independent record stores located usually in urban areas of the United States and specializing (at least partly) in hard core rap records which are sold mostly through word of mouth.

It was eventually determined that the harder the core of an underground rap record, the bigger the unit sales and the more income the artist and the record label would earn. The underground record market established the fact that there exists an enormous audience (comprised mostly of youthful record buyers) which apparently enjoys hard core rap. Moreover, this consumer group is not limited to African-American youth who live in America's African-American ghettos. Record industry sales research indicates that roughly sixty percent of all rap records sold are bought by whites. The form known as Gangsta Rap is a relatively recent spin-off of basic hard core. Gangsta Rap lyrics tend to glorify or glamorize rebelliousness, defiance of the law or various forms of street "hustling" in the minds of the listeners, much the same way as being "hard" and "tough" has historically been and still is being glamorized in the movies and often times on television.

As to the question: "Why would African-American youth be so receptive to the marketing of hard core and Gangsta Rap and the messages within?" I would ask: "Why wouldn't African-American youth pay attention to artists who seem to fully understand the lifestyle problems that African-American youth face. And why wouldn't African-American youth be anxious to listen to recording artists who are willing to openly discuss and dramatize many of these dire problems within the context of their records?" Please keep in mind that, for the most part, these are African-American youth for whom America has shown no real concern—at least during the past decade or more. These are African-American youth in whom our country has invested very little over the past decade in terms of channeling economic assistance and better training and education.

Over the last decade, our country has invested almost nothing toward creating the kinds of opportunity which would allow such citizens to eventually better their lives, their surroundings and ultimately their futures as Americans. I tend to wonder if we shouldn't be far more concerned about eliminating poverty, violence, despair and hopelessness from low income African-American communities than about eliminating Gangsta Rap. In spite of its many critics and detractors, rap music has, indeed, been very effective and in some ways a Godsend in providing entertainment relief and in many cases economic relief to a largely forgotten community. On the other hand, it goes without saying that anyone who sells any form of entertainment which is either anti-social or illegal in nature and cannot be indulged in except behind closed doors, is engaged in what could be defined as pandering. This same standard should also apply regarding hard core or Gangsta Rap.

Therefore, any recording artist or record label who creates or sells any record which is anti-social, profane, violent or sexually explicit in nature to such a degree that it cannot be listened to in public without offending others or cannot be listened to by youthful fans of such music in the presence of an adult authority figure, in a certain sense, is also engaged in pandering. I recently heard a well known Gangsta rapper explain his philosophy during a TV interview. He said, "I make music for poor people and there are far more poor people than rich people! So, as long as I satisfy poor people, I'll always have a job!"

I viewed this explanation as quite intelligent and well thought out; but clearly a case of pandering to the naivete of youthful record buyers who are intrigued by anti-social commentary. At this time I am not prepared to say which is more perverse between pandering by certain political ideologues who do it to appease those who are turned on by pro–law and order, anti-urban development, anti-welfare and tax cutting rhetoric or pandering by recording artists and record companies to youth who think it's hip to listen to Gangsta Rap. If I were asked, "Should governmental steps be taken to curtail hard core or Gangsta Rap; or to clean up rap lyrics; or to make recording artists or record companies pandering to the rebelliousness of youth illegal," I would say no to all three. Consumer pandering within reason is, of course, an accepted practice in America with respect to entertainment distribution. Movie studios and home video movie distributors openly pander to customers who enjoy somewhat anti-social or sexually explicit entertainment.

Most major distributors of such entertainment do, however, exercise a reasonable degree of social responsibility through the almost universal use of a well designed rating system. Rap music does not need to be censored. Rap music and all other recordings do need to be rated just as movies are. Records by recording artists which are violently or sexually explicit or which promote illegal (drug or firearm use or and other anti-social behavior) should be clearly marked and identified "X-rated." The "parental guidance" sticker system presently being used in the recording industry is simply not enough. The MPAA (Motion Picture Association of America) rating system allowed the movie industry to separate exploiters and panderers from legitimately creative filmmakers. The same result can occur with regard to the music industry with the support and participation of the RIAA (Record Industry Association of America).

As the situation now stands, there is no real stigma attached to the creation, marketing or advertising of a profane or anti-social record or LP. Individuals and companies which now openly pander to youth consumers who are attracted to anti-social recorded product would market such product with far less pride of accomplishment in the face of a strong rating system. A strong rating system will also place somewhat of a stigma on consumer ownership of such product regardless of the consumer's age. While a rating system may not completely solve all of the problems concerning hard core or Gangsta Rap recordings, such a process may be well worth considering as a place to begin. Thank you.

A blowup of the sexually suggestive cartoon album cover to Snoop's 1993 album *Doggystyle* was on a stand, an illustration of the nastiness that gangsta rap represented. Despite Cornelius's harsh words for gangsta rap, Snoop Dogg never lost his love for *Soul Train*. When asked about the show's impact on him growing up in Long Beach, Snoop had a unique perspective. He said, "A lot of my homies, when we go to jail, we measure our time by how many *Soul Train*s you got left. I got my five *Soul Train*s. That means you're getting out in five weeks. I got seven *Soul Train*s left—I'm getting out in seven weeks. As sad as it is, it was a good feeling because when you in jail, you had to have something to keep you up, and *Soul Train* kept a lot of brothers up. That was the main effect they had on Long Beach that I remember."

It was just this kind of jailhouse perspective that made gangsta rap popular and everyone in the black music mainstream uncomfortable. But Cornelius, being a businessman, would have Snoop on episode #743 in 1993 to perform "What's My Name" from that same *Doggystyle* album, which won best album at the 1994 Soul Train Awards. Snoop made a very heartfelt tribute to the show: "I ain't mad 'cause I didn't win no Grammy. This is the black folks' Grammys!"

Throughout the late 1980s and beyond, those clean versions of rap songs by Snoop and others made it possible for *Soul Train*, as well as radio stations, to play some of the hooky but hard-core rap hits of the day. But true hip-hop fans knew that what they heard on TV was the watered-down version, and that the lip-synched performances on the show were inferior to the kinetic music videos in rotation on MTV, BET, and elsewhere. Don's discomfort with gangsta rap haunted the show, so despite its commercial viability, its graphic content really made it inappropriate daytime-TV fare. This wasn't the O'Jays or Al Green. The times had changed. Hip-hop wasn't Cornelius's music and never would be.

DANCER PROFILE: Rosie Perez

Rosie Perez came out to sun-kissed California from Bushwick, Brooklyn, a burnt-out, impoverished neighborhood in a tattered borough, bringing a fierce warrior attitude that was reflected in her take-no-prisoners dancing. Short and curvy with reddish hair, pouty lips, and a high-pitched voice with a thick Nuyorican accent, Perez was a unique and, to some, disquieting presence on the *Soul Train* set.

"Rosie came on the show, and she was just so hot and so sexy," Crystal McCarey said. "That girl could dance. She could move. You know, females will be females. They're catty. When Rosie came, I think that some of the other dancers were a bit intimidated, and they weren't friendly or kind to her."

McCarey befriended the new girl and advised her not to worry about what the other dancers thought of her. "Rosie was a very sweet lady, but she was one hell of a dancer. I would have to say that I thought I was hot stuff, too, but when I saw Rosie, I was like, Oh, my goodness. She got that fire."

It wasn't only women who had complicated feelings about the Brooklynite. The Cutty mack himself, Louie "Ski" Carr, would sometimes let Rosie and some other dancers stay at his apartment on weekends *Soul Train* was taped. "Her girls and her used to change, sleep over, and go to the next show," Carr said. That sense of fellowship didn't always translate to the studio. "We was cool, but on the *Train* it was a chance to just be yourself and do your thing. She was doing her thing, and I was doing my thing. There's actual footage of us boogying and having that friendly competitiveness. Rosie was aggressive and sexy and a little street, like a machine gun. Just do her move strong. Men love strong women, plus she's beautiful."

Rosie Perez's fierce New York–styled dancing made her an immediate fan favorite.

Perez's *Soul Train* career began, like so many others, at a Los Angeles nightclub. The nineteen-year-old had initially come west to help a struggling cousin with her two young children. When that arrangement proved too stressful, Rosie began working part-time jobs while attending classes in three different LA-area universities as a biochemistry major. She got some stability when she landed a job working as secretary and babysitter for the family behind Golden Bird fried chicken.

Along with some girlfriends, Rosie was at a club called Florentine Gardens when Chuck Johnson inquired if she'd like to be on the show. Skeptical New Yorker to her core, Rosie replied, "Yeah, right." Johnson said, "No, really," and handed her his card. She remembers standing on the floor at Florentine Gardens "screaming my head off. I was like, *Ahhh!* To be so young and being a teenager, being asked to go on *Soul Train*, it was just—it was mind-blowing. He said, Will you come, will you show up on Saturday? I said, Can my girlfriends come? And he said, What do they look like? I thought that was so rude. Thank God they were hot. So we all got to go, and that's how I got on *Soul Train*."

"The first time I went on," she continued, "it was bittersweet because I did not know that we were going to be waiting outside of the gates of the studio and jockeying for position. I was like, 'Oh, we're outta here.' We were about to leave. The talent scout from *Soul Train* was like, 'No, no, no, you, short one. Come in.' I said, 'Well, I'm not coming unless all my girlfriends get in.' That was great, but it wasn't great for me because he let us in, we didn't have to wait on line. So when the rest of the people came in, instant hatred. It was really crazy." That introduction to the show was likely the root of the disdain McCarey spoke about. "There was really great people," Perez said, "but there were a few that were real bitter."

Like most popular *Soul Train* dancers, Rosie Perez was the toast of LA parties.

Perez, who had come from a New York City street dance aesthetic where unisex sportswear was the norm, arrived at the studio in jeans, sneakers, and a T-shirt, and staffers told her it wasn't proper *Soul Train* attire. Instead they pointed out a girl in a super-short dress. Rosie had wisely brought a sexier change of clothes. Not only did they like what she'd changed into, but the producers immediately placed Rosie on a riser, where the camera was sure to find her.

Don selected Perez to do the *Soul Train* scramble board, yet another honor for the novice. When Rosie spoke in that now famous Brooklyn-meets–Puerto Rico accent the host asked her, "Is that how you really talk?" Embarrassed, Perez did her best to lose the accent. Perez's good fortune, not having to wait in line and getting a riser spot on her first day, made the New Yorker a target for some old heads on the set.

> **Perez:** I think that the girls were jealous because of that. We were all very, very young. Not only the girls there were jealous. There was also boys that were jealous, and these were people who saw *Soul Train* as a springboard to further success. I did not view it that way. I just viewed it as "Oh my God, we're on *Soul Train*!" In hindsight I understood why they were jealous. I don't know if it was jealous as much as angry, because they were on *Soul Train* for years and years and years, and these kids, they used to practice for hours, their dance moves, their dance routines, what they were gonna do going down the *Soul Train* line. They would spend hours picking out their outfits.

Though viewers and other dancers characterize Perez as an aggressive dancer, she feels that she held back while on the show.

Perez: Don Cornelius did not want to see how I really danced—I was doing hip-hop, and it was foreign to people out in California. They only knew about popping and locking, so they were not keen on hip-hop dancing. Don was like, "No, no, no. You're a girl." I was like, What? This is really weird. Then I had to dance in high heels, and I never danced in high heels before, and I had this little tiny short dress, and it's riding up my ass and I'm like, Oh my God. I couldn't move. As you can see from the tapes, I had absolutely no style whatsoever on that show. The first couple of times, I didn't know what the hell I was doing. I was just excited and nervous and scared and just elated. That was my style. A bunch of nerves just oozing out of my body.

Whenever Rosie was in doubt about her moves, she would "face dance, just face dance. Face dance means you don't know what the hell the rest of your body was doing but your face is *fierce*. That's face dancing." Perez is much harder on herself than she needs to be. Anyone who saw her on *Soul Train* was impressed with her dancing. Most people who remember her from the show usually recall her dancing in either a red or black dress. That wasn't part of any plan. They were just the only dressy clothes this college student owned.

"Your attire had to feel like you were going to a nightclub," Perez said. "That's the look that they wanted, and they wanted high fashion, which I did not offer because I could only afford a dress that had that much material. I was very proud of my body back then. That's the other thing I loved. I was hot. It's good, it's on tape forever. Yeah, you look like you were having a night out. That was another great thing about *Soul Train*. I have a picture of all of us going to a club with my friends from *Soul Train*. All the girls just going out to a nightclub, and we're all dressed like we were dressed on *Soul Train*. It was the most surreal experience for me because I walk into the club with them and people started screaming. 'Oh my God! It's the *Soul Train* dancers!' It was really weird."

When you see Rosie in *Soul Train* footage on YouTube, she is coming down the *Soul Train* line like an unleashed tiger. Her first time down the line was, for her, the most memorable:

Perez: I was hysterical. My heart was pounding. I didn't know what I was going to do. A lot of the dancers already had their routine worked out ahead of time, and I'm just freaking out. I don't know what to do, and then you stand at the head of the line, and then, and the stage manager goes, "*Go!*" It was ridiculous, it was so bad. My girlfriends were cracking up at me because I'm hilarious, and I have a great sense of humor. I was laughing at myself. By the time I got to the end of the line, I was just in hysterics. I was laughing so hard, and Don Cornelius goes, "Do it again." What? "Do it again. Put her up at the head of the line." And I thought I had messed up, so I did something different and Don goes, "No, no, no, do it again. Do exactly what you did the first time."

What Perez thought was silly Don loved, which speaks to their difference in perspective about what good dancing was.

Much like Jody Watley and other popular *Soul Train* dancers, her sudden TV celebrity led to a lot of real-world hostility. "I used to get recognized quite often as being a *Soul Train* dancer," Rosie said. "Quite often. Which was great at times but sometimes was not so great. Especially back at college it was not so great. It was pretty tough."

A turning point in her relationship with *Soul Train* came when Don tried to recruit Perez into a female vocal trio along with Cheryl Song and a white dancer-singer. "I told Don I could carry a tune, but I couldn't *sing* sing, you know. He told me, 'It's irrelevant the way you sing. What's relevant is the way you dance and the way you wear your clothes.'" That didn't exactly charm Perez. Nor did the fact that when he handed her a contract, she was told not to contact an attorney. No negotiation. He wanted her to sign the contract immediately. On the heels of multicultural hit making by the Mary Jane Girls and Vanity 6, Cornelius was clearly seeing Perez and company as a solid bet.

But she still refused to sign the deal, so in an attempt to woo her, Don took her out to dinner. A business meal turned social as, for the first time, he inquired about her background and family. "What broke the ice was that when we sat down, I didn't know which fork to use," Perez recalled with a laugh. "Don said, 'Work outside in.' And then he cracked up. I cracked up, too. It was the first time I saw him laugh." The duo had a lovely meal except for one thing—Perez still wouldn't sign the contract.

That cordial meal was followed by a tense taping in which the host stopped Perez "three or four times" as she grooved down the *Soul Train* line. Unlike her first time, when Don made her go back, his tone was harsh. During a break, the two had a confrontation over the record deal and, according to Perez, she tossed one of the handy fried chicken boxes at him and stormed off the soundstage. That was the last time she'd dance on the show.

But this dustup with Don wouldn't be the end of Perez's relationship with *Soul Train*. About a year before Rosie was banned from dancing on the show, Louil Silas, a vice president for R&B A&R at MCA Records, was visiting the show with an artist when he spotted Rosie dancing in a corner by herself.

"I was on the side and I started dancing hip-hop," Rosie said. "Louil came over and said, 'What's that dance? What is that?

What are you doing right there?' I said, 'Oh, that's hip-hop.' He goes, 'Hip-hop, hip-hop, cool. Yeah, that's what I want.' I said, 'Huh?' He said, 'Bobby Brown [of New Edition] is going solo. I want you to teach him that.' I said, 'I'm not a choreographer.' He goes, 'I'll pay you sixteen hundred dollars.' I go, 'I'll be there on Monday.' That was the beginning of my choreography career. That's how it all started. It started from *Soul Train*."

In the mid- to late eighties, when hip-hop-bred dance moves from the East Coast began to overturn the West Coast styles popularized on *Soul Train* in the seventies, Perez became a bridge between the two worlds. Videos were slowly beginning to replace *Soul Train* as the place where new dances went national. Bobby Brown, probably a more gifted dancer than singer, was the first of many acts Perez began choreographing for videos, TV appearances, and tours.

After working with Brown, she designed steps for kiddie group the Boys, the agile rapper Heavy D of Heavy D and the Boyz, LL Cool J, and new jack swing groups Today and Wreckx-n-Effect. She even worked with the ultimate diva, Diana Ross. But the gig that put her career over the top was selecting and choreographing the Fly Girls for Keenen Ivory Wayans's sketch comedy show *In Living Color* on Fox. On the show, which debuted in April 1990, the four dancers under Rosie's guidance became the new cutting edge of urban dance. It was the peak of her career as a choreographer.

"I was busy," Perez recalled fondly. "I had a great career, and it all stemmed from being on *Soul Train*, which is crazy. It's really, really crazy."

That's how her *Soul Train* story comes full circle. As a choreographer, Perez became an occasional visitor to the set, aiding artists she was working with on steps for their TV appearance. At first Cornelius was prickly, and later he just ignored her. A few years later, after her acting in Spike Lee's *Do the Right Thing* and working on *In Living Color,* the two ran into each other in the tunnel underneath an LA concert venue. At first Perez ignored him, but he called out to her.

"I apologized for tossing the chicken at him," Perez said, "and I thanked him for giving me such a great platform. He told me how talented I was and how proud he was of me. We hugged and smiled. I saw the guy from our dinner at that moment. Then he told me not to tell anyone about it: 'After all, I have an image to maintain.'"

Chapter 13
OVERSEAS SOUL

||||||||||||||||||||||||||||||||||||||

EVERYONE WHO danced on *Soul Train* and did any traveling to Europe or Asia had to be prepared for the excitement of being recognized by people in another country who spoke a different language. But the show's international appeal didn't always sit so well with its founder.

Cornelius: Well, as far as *Soul Train*'s popularity outside the United States goes, we've never been able to gauge it so far. What we know so far is that most people outside the US that carry *Soul Train* are not paying anybody. They are not paying for the show, and that takes us back to some of the money that we weren't able to make. There are so many ways to get—from YouTube on down—to get copies of intellectual property and then use it, that it's become impossible to keep track of.

Any quick trip around the Internet in 2013 will find some legally licensed *Soul Train* content (the *Soul Train* Japan website is owned by

Soul Train Holdings) and plenty of unofficial events (for example, a party in March 2013 in Bristol, England). But during Cornelius's lifetime, episodes of the show, many posted from Japan, proliferated. Jody Watley recalls that in the seventies there was a special *Soul Train* taping for Japanese TV, a suggestion that Cornelius had tried to do business overseas, but apparently it didn't ripen into a deal.

For many years after Watley started her recording career, she'd wanted to use vintage footage of herself as a *Soul Train* dancer in her live show, but Cornelius's company could never accommodate her. However, a trip to Japan changed that. "I did a show in Tokyo in the eighties," Watley said, "and after the show, these girls gave me a VHS that was filled with highlights of every damn number I did on *Soul Train*. I have no idea how they collected all that footage."

Soul Train maniac Ahmir Thompson had a similar experience when he traveled to Japan with the Roots in 1996. "I met a fan, and he had two hundred to three hundred episodes from the seventies," said Thompson.

This Japanese interest in black music, while not widespread across the country, was deep for those who loved it. For a time there was a *Soul Train* Club in Japan, as well as nightclubs named after Motown Records and the Apollo Theater—all venues dedicated to the hard-core soul music fan.

Because of the complexity of licensing deals, Cornelius was limited in exploiting the shows internationally, but via VHS, DVD, and, eventually, the Internet, *Soul Train* was an international presence from its earliest days. *Soul Train* was incredibly popular in Japan, where the Japanese—great consumers of all aspects of black musical culture—would bring over dancers from the show starting in the late seventies (and still do into the twenty-first century).

It's not surprising that the show's one Asian dance star, Cheryl Song, was invited over along with three black dancers. More amusing is her experience there.

The female dancers of *Soul Train* brought beauty, style, and creativity to the weekly broadcasts.

Song: Nobody recognized me. I remember we rehearsed and we rehearsed and rehearsed. I helped make a lot of the costumes. When we got to Japan, it was four of us—three black dancers and me. Everybody would come and talk to me. Not because they thought I was the dancer with the long hair—they thought I was the tour guide! They thought I was the translator! So, you know, we were in Japan, and I'm not even Japanese! They would always come to me and *speak Japanese*, and I was like, "What?" And that happened to me a lot. So believe me, that knocked me down to the ground. I didn't believe I was popular, I didn't think I was all that. That kind of brought me back to reality.

In 1985 Derek Fleming—also known as Dfox—took another trip over to Japan with Song, along with Ricky Carson and Nieci Payne.

"Recognition in another country is just unbelievable," Fleming said. "It was everything you can imagine."

On that tour the four dancers were over in Japan for two months performing every night, but Mondays at a club called the Latin Quarters. While in Japan the quartet hung out at a spot called Club Temps. Fleming said, "I'll never forget being there. We walk in, and we had no idea *Soul Train* would be playing on the monitors. But then almost every club we went into in Japan was showing *Soul Train* on the monitors."

Nieci Payne, who was on that tour with Fleming and Song, actually learned to speak Japanese. As a result she'd go back and forth between the United States and Japan for almost ten years. She felt "*Soul Train* in Osaka and Tokyo was bigger than the show here. I remember going down the street, and some kids going, '*Soul Train* dancer.' So you literally found yourself signing autographs daily." Payne got modeling gigs in Japan and danced with American bands on tour there. "A lot of people went to Japan from the show and still live there from America because of dancing on *Soul Train*."

In 2004 Jody Watley had an unexpected *Soul Train* moment in Malaysia. She had traveled over with other international artists to do a benefit concert in the wake of the tsunami's devastation of the country. "After the speeches and the food, when the music started, just two songs in, they wanted to do a *Soul Train* line. I just had to laugh. [The show] was something that had such a positive impact on so many people, and you may not realize what that impact is."

So while Don Cornelius may have felt ripped off by the show's online ubiquity, *Soul Train*'s global impact can't be quantified in dollars and cents.

DANCER PROFILE: Marco De Santiago

Marco De Santiago was one of the most colorful and enduring *Soul Train* dancers. He was a lean, handsome, big-haired man with a distinctive fashion sense who appeared on the show from 1976 to 1993, going from the days of disco to the height of new jack swing. When he was in the eleventh grade, De Santiago was attending a Saturday-morning high school track meet when a comely cheerleader asked if he'd like to attend *Soul Train* with her. De Santiago's reaction? "I thought, 'Oh my God. I don't like cameras. I don't like TV. I don't want any part of it.'"

So De Santiago tried to avoid her, but the cheerleader was persistent and insisted that he come and pick her up. Reluctantly he swung by in his car, and they drove over to KTTV Studios in Hollywood. "So we go there," he recalled, "and I'm thinking I don't even know what to do. Nor did she. We don't see a sign that says *Soul Train* or anything. So a guy comes over and says, 'Okay, you two follow me.' I thought we're in trouble. They're gonna call my mother. I don't know what's gonna happen when we go inside. There was *Soul Train*. Here I was just a guy in school, and to see these glamorous people and these girls. It was just so exciting. But I could see the camera, and I would be like, 'Don't face the camera.' So I would turn my back."

But De Santiago's hair, cut into a massive Afro, overshadowed his modesty. A member of the production staff came over and suggested that he use Afro Sheen on his hair. "We would just buy the cheap products," he admitted, "but the Johnson Products people were like, 'We want this guy.'" De Santiago and his cheerleader date ended up doing the scramble board. At that time folks who did the scramble board got two gifts: a Panasonic eight-track player and a box of Fashion Fair cosmetics. When the box of makeup arrived at the De Santiago household, his mother had a moment of concern. "So she says, 'I noticed a box came for you, and there is makeup inside. Is there anything you want to tell me?'"

While his mother's fears about her son's post–*Soul Train* sexuality were unfounded, De Santiago definitely found his status at high school forever altered by his appearances on the broadcast. "You sort of obtain all these friends that you didn't know were your friends, like the football players, the jocks," he said. "I won't say the teachers were kinder, but the security guards weren't exactly as bossy, and you suddenly had a few more dates than you would have had . . . What was even more interesting was the nonblacks recognized me from *Soul Train*. *Soul Train* came on local TV after *The Twilight Zone* and before *I Love Lucy*, so the *Twilight Zone* fans recognized me and the *I Love Lucy* fans recognized me."

De Santiago was becoming a celebrity via *Soul Train* but his family didn't have a TV, which is probably hard for folks born in the media-saturated twenty-first century to believe. But into the 1970s there were many families, either because of financial or religious reasons, who didn't own a set. One Saturday De Santiago and a friend drove out to the Northridge Mall, went into the Sears, and turned all the store's TVs to *Soul Train* so they could finally see the show. Word got around the mall that a *Soul Train* dancer was in Sears, and a spooked De Santiago had to make a hasty retreat while being followed by twenty-five excited high school girls.

Why was De Santiago so recognizable? When he first danced on *Soul Train*, the teen had a huge Afro, not atypical of the time. But in the late 1970s, he altered his hairstyle and picked up the nickname "the Black Barry Gibb." "I used to wear my hair blow-dried and feathered," he said. "Some people call it my Revlon days—meaning my Revlon perm." The best reference point for De Santiago's hair were the flowing locks of Bee Gees singer Barry Gibb on the cover of their *Spirits Having Flown* album. "All the attention made me more polite with people and more patient," he says. "I was gonna have to talk to people, so it made me more comfortable talking more."

Along with his elaborate hair, De Santiago dressed in a style hard to miss. "In the earlier days it was really common for couples to match up," he said. So he'd talk with longtime dance partner Dina Rivera either during the week or on the Friday night before a Saturday taping about coordinating clothes. Usually she set the tone, telling him what colors she was wearing. Sometimes De Santiago scrambled to a mall at its ten A.M. opening time before an eleven A.M. taping to grab a shirt—or to quickly spray-paint one to alter its color.

De Santiago, like many *Soul Train* regulars, learned how to "Hollywood" his clothes, using safety pins and tape to make oversize garments fit or to cover tears created by rigorous dancing. Unlike today, when designers and brands would have been aggressive in trying to get *Soul Train* dancers to wear their gear, in the seventies no major brands sought to dress them. So they had to become crafty shoppers at stores like Macy's, Bloomingdale's, and Neiman Marcus, always looking for sale items around the time of *Soul Train* tapings.

But De Santiago didn't hit his stride as a dresser until he matured, along with *Soul Train*, in the mid-eighties. "After we became more comfortable being there, we felt that we had an obligation," he said. "We don't have to wear what's local. So how do we stay ahead?" He and his friends turned to Italian and French *Vogue*, as well as *Gentleman's Quarterly*, to upgrade their gear and be fashion forward. "If we filmed in September, by the time the taping came on in December maybe those fashions had come out," he recalled. Tuxedos, cummerbunds, sashes around his waist, and scarves were all aspects of his dress game.

In 1986 De Santiago was in a car accident. A leg was shattered into forty-five pieces. In an earlier era, the leg would have been amputated. Instead he was given a choice: either a body cast for a year or a metal rod in the leg for a year and a half. He chose the rod. "That was the longest year and a half of my life because I love to dance so much. Once I learned how to walk again, I went to *Soul Train*," he recalled. It was some time in 1987 when he showed up on the set. Don and the production team hadn't known what happened to him.

After being told the story, Don, Chuck Johnson, and his team invited De Santiago to dance on a riser. "Someone helps me up there and I'm dancing. One of the funniest things about it is someone said, 'Wow, you're really dancing really well.' I said, 'You have no idea how much pain I'm in.' My leg did not bend. The screws were large. You can't imagine trying to dance with screws in your body." But that wasn't the end of the day.

De Santiago was then invited to dance down the *Soul Train* line. He'd never really enjoyed the line when healthy, but everyone wanted to try it. "I don't even have a word for it. But that many people liked or respected me, who were glad I was back. So I go down the line and I hear people say, 'Go Marco! Go Marco!' It was so encouraging." Looking at video of that moment on line, he "could see the facial expression. I had to look to see if I was bleeding at all. I thought, I'm gonna always remember that everyone was just so happy I was back."

For De Santiago, who had one of the longest runs of any dancer on the show, the golden age of *Soul Train* was not the seventies but late eighties and early nineties. "There were groups like Tony! Toni! Toné! or Guy that were this perfect marriage of hip-hop and R&B. It was really exciting at that time. But I felt like, Okay, I thought it was time for me to leave. Leave this to the young ones. Leave it to the sixteen-year-olds, just as I was sixteen years old."

Today he works as an analyst at a cancer laboratory, working as a middleman between doctors and scientists when someone is diagnosed with the disease. That's his day job. But *Soul Train* remains a huge part of his life. De Santiago has become a key organizer of gatherings of the early *Soul Train* dancers. He put together a memorial for Don Cornelius at Maverick's Flat after Don's passing, and for Labor Day weekend in 2013 he organized three days of events in Los Angeles featuring *Soul Train* dancers.

Chapter 14
SEX AND *SOUL TRAIN*

||||||||||||||||||||||||||||||||

ROMANCE AND dancing. They go together better than chicken and waffles—whether it's in an inner-city basement or a country-and-western hoedown. Combine that basic law of nature with the legendarily hypersexual atmosphere of Los Angeles in the 1970s and '80s, and, as you'd expect, there were many sexscapades inspired by the *Soul Train* experience.

Derek Fleming, also known as Dfox, loved the dating scene around the show. "A lot of us were dating at the time the shooting went on," he said. "You would see split-ups, and that's why you wouldn't see a certain person dancing with another person. I ran into Otis Williams of the Temptations in the hall, and I told him I went out with his daughter. Her name was Lana. A beautiful girl. A Playboy Bunny. I dated some stars. I won't say those names."

Over the course of his long tenure on *Soul Train*, Marco De Santiago would be engaged (though never married) to three different women he met on Don's dance floor. "I had three close calls," he says, "all with *Soul Train* girls. The dating scene was very competitive. But it wasn't just dancer versus dancer. Your competition for a girl on that show would also be Magic Johnson or Keith Sweat. I was trying to talk to a girl on the show but then I saw Smokey Robinson give her his phone number. Tough to compete against Smokey."

Don Cornelius, in his wisdom, did his best to discourage his dancers, particularly his young, barely legal female dancers, from hooking up with the singers and musicians who performed on the show. He didn't want *Soul Train* viewed as a pickup spot or a home base for groupies. It was a very practical but extremely difficult—damn near impossible—rule to enforce. The women of *Soul Train* would, in fact, prove to be muses for some of the greatest songwriters of the era. Reportedly Robinson wrote his sensual "The Agony and the Ecstasy" from his classic *A Quiet Storm* album about a *Soul Train* dancer. Marvin Gaye would go further, writing much of his landmark *I Want You* album about a seventeen-year-old woman named Jan he met at the show and would subsequently marry.

One of the chief violators of Don's rules to keep male singers away from his young female dancers would be Charlie Wilson, the charismatic, ultrasoulful lead singer of the Gap Band. His father had been a preacher and, like a lot of children of ministers, Wilson was drawn to the wild side of life.

"Growing up in Oklahoma, my mother said we weren't allowed to listen to blues music in the house," Wilson remembered. "But we'd go around to the next-door neighbor's on Saturday for *Soul Train*. Man, it was incredible. I just said, I want to one day do that. I remember saying, I wanna do that. Seeing Stevie Wonder on *Soul Train*. I wanted to do that. It was incredible. *Soul Train* showed me this is what I'm gonna do."

The sex appeal of the *Soul Train* dancers was crucial to the show's success.

Wilson grew up relatively sheltered in Tulsa in a tight-knit, church-based community. He sang gospel in church as a teenager, but he also started slipping out to nightclubs, first on the mostly black north side of Tulsa and then the south side, which was where white bands performed. So in 1967 Wilson, along with his two brothers, Ronnie and Robert, formed a group, the Gap Band (named after the Tulsa streets Greenwood, Archer, and Pine), that quickly became one of the most popular bands in the city. They got their first record deal while living in Tulsa but didn't hit their stride until they moved to Los Angeles and became part of the Crenshaw Boulevard scene that incubated so many *Soul Train* dancers. Lonnie Simmons, who'd later sign them to his Total Experience Records, also owned a cool nightclub with the same name.

Wilson: I remember pulling up in front of the Total Experience nightclub. There were Rolls-Royces lined in front. I remember seeing a black one with maroon piping. I remember seeing a tan one and I remember seeing another kind of foreign car. The crowd was lined up around the corner. It was definitely a place I really wanted to go into and see what all the hoopla was about. The moment I stepped in the place, it was jam-packed, and the Dramatics was performing. It was crazy. I remember there were three clubs on that particular street: at the front was Maverick's Flat, in the middle was the Pied Piper, and then there was the Total Experience. It seemed like in order to get where you needed to go, or if you needed to get to the big one, you had to get into Maverick's Flat. If you could get into Maverick's Flat and be seen and be accepted, then you were on your way. It was like a gateway into the music business. It took a long time for us to get in there. We wanted to play our own music. Stuff that we had written, and it was like, "Well, where's your Top Forty stuff at?" So we had to go back. First they said you have to have Top Forty, play Top Forty—what is your original stuff? So we went back and wrote the original stuff. It was like they were tricking us. They didn't want us in the club. It was a weird deal, but we went in there one day and performed for those guys and just lit the place on fire. It was amazing during that time. The club scene was hot.

Backed by Total Experience, who'd recently signed a distribution deal with PolyGram Records, the Gap Band would establish themselves as a viable band with the P-Funk-derivative cut "I Don't Believe You Want to Get Up and Dance (Oops!)" in 1979. They made their *Soul Train* debut on episode #320 as the secondary act to Shalamar.

Wilson: Man, I was nervous. First time on *Soul Train*! We was all nervous. I know I was shaking. Don Cornelius had to come backstage and said, "Listen, just calm down. It's all good. It's just like how you perform. I watch you perform all the time." I was talking to him just shaking, and he grabbed me, and I was still shaking. Don was like, "You're really nervous! Just calm down, it's gonna be all right." We got up there and did our song "Shake." I thought I was gonna forget my steps. The place came unglued when we went onstage, and it just made me feel a little bit calmer. Had a good time that day. Don Cornelius, he really calmed me down a lot. I was mostly scared of being on the stage with him walking up to me to talk to me. He was the one to calm me down in the beginning. He came, had a conversation with me. I was like, "Okay, he's just a man." I can't remember what our conversation was about. But we had a conversation and he just calmed my spirit down. Don Cornelius was like the cornerstone of black music. He was the launching pad for anybody that was successful. He was part of the reason—definitely was part of the reason why you were successful. It was his show, and his creation that made things work for you, and it was sort of hard getting on Don Cornelius, but if he liked the record, then it was on. If the record was responding, it was on. He would put you in if the record was responding. If it wasn't responding, then you just, you didn't get the good look. It was like it is like now, but he was definitely the gatekeeper. But he gave everybody a shot that deserved a shot.

Once Wilson got comfortable on the *Soul Train* stage, coming back often in the 1980s with an impressive string of hits with the Gap Band, he became very confident in approaching the dancers.

Wilson: We weren't allowed to dance with the people on the shows—we were not allowed to do that. Don would not have allowed them to have any association with the artist and the camaraderie. None of that. They were not allowed to do that. So we were definitely parted on the stage, and the crowd was just partying anyway. It's just as though we were right next to them. I can reach down and touch them. They would definitely go for it. They weren't supposed to, but we always would break all the rules as entertainers. After those *Soul Train* shows, there were definitely some beautiful women up there, man. I was not married then. Well, after the show the place was packed full of young men and beautiful women. We definitely went through the audience to get back to the stage, and on your way to the dressing room you would eye and find the one you was gonna talk to. We'd been through taping in about thirty minutes. We used to go from *Soul Train* to the clubs. We would take a carload of maybe fifteen. We had a good time. A good time. Guys would pile a limousine up with everybody, and there were definitely some beautiful women in the car.

I definitely got a few dates out of *Soul Train*. I had some fun. Met three girls in there and I had a long relationship with each one of them. Maybe three years one, three years another one. I was talking to Don and saying thank you. Then me trying to get through the crowd was tedious. I was mobbed. Maybe the first girl who grabbed me was one who I ended up seeing for a while. It was something to behold.

Other male entertainers interviewed about *Soul Train* weren't as frank as Charlie Wilson about their sexual conquests. Time and, perhaps, current marriages put a damper on that line of storytelling. But a couple performers enjoyed real love stories because of the show.

Tomi Jenkins of Cameo and *Soul Train* dancer Nieci Payne did their VH1 documentary interview together, a testament to their ongoing relationship of some twenty-plus years. Jenkins has been a working musician since joining a thirteen-member band called the New York City Players in 1974. Subsequently they changed their name to Cameo and in 1976 signed to Casablanca Records, where they had a successful run as a large funk band.

In the early 1980s, when live horns and traditional rhythm sections gave way to synthesizers and drum machines, Cameo shrank down to three key members and overhauled its sound, entering an innovative period of music and videos that peaked with the 1985 single "Word Up!" that Jenkins cowrote. Jenkins, along with the group's leader Larry Blackmon, still record and tour to this day. As strong a career as Jenkins has had in music, he's not nearly as legendary as Nieci Payne. Quite simply, Payne is the Brick House. In old-school black slang, a "brick house" was a woman with incredible curves and an imposing stature. As a young woman in LA, Payne was seen by the Commodores, who wrote the classic funk jam "Brick House" (with the famous line "36-24-36, what a winning hand!") about her statuesque frame.

The sexy dancer's connection to *Soul Train* goes back to the post–Don Cornelius daily shows in Chicago, on which she danced as a high schooler in the late 1970s. In fact, in a dance contest run by Chicago host Clinton Ghent, Payne won a pair of shoes from a shoe store owned by Chaka Khan. After graduating from high school, she headed west to try and get on the national broadcast. Many have talked about the challenges of getting on the show, but it wasn't a problem for Payne. At an LA club she met veteran *Soul Train* dancer Thelma Davis, who, after checking out Payne's moves, invited the young woman to a *Soul Train* taping.

"I wore tie-dye pants—they were elephant pants—a T-shirt, and these two Afro puffs," she said. "I went on there, and Don Cornelius saw me dancing on the floor. When he introduced himself to me, I said,

'Don, I'm from Chicago,' and he said, 'Cool. Cool. Let's see what you can do,' and I rocked it for eleven years, from 1980 to 1991." Jenkins, already a music-business veteran, first saw Payne on the show. "She was always on the platform," he remembered. He wasn't the only music-business figure to notice her. During her tenure on *Soul Train*, she'd be recruited by the Commodores, the Emotions, Con Funk Shun, L.T.D., and Rose Royce to perform on tours and other TV shows.

Within the world of *Soul Train*, as we've noted, Don tried to keep his young dancers away from each other. And, as Charlie Wilson made clear, that didn't always work out. "We would go in the back and take pictures, and a lot of times celebrities would take pictures," Payne said. "It was kind of a no-no to do." Yet away from the set, Don would have dinners where he, the dancers, and the artists could mingle.

Payne: Don went to dinner, and he would call me from time to time and say, "Nieci, I'm going to dinner. Do you and a couple of girls wanna go out and eat dinner with me and some friends?" It would usually be like a group. But it was just straight. Let's have dinner. Everybody leave. Bye. It wasn't like you get there and hooked up with somebody. It wasn't that kind of story. Tomi was there when we had dinner at Tramps of London. It was a club out here in the Beverly Center at the time. We all had dinner, and it was right before it was time to go, and he said, 'Hey, you wanna go out?' No, actually, what Tomi said was, 'You don't want to go out with me, do you?' I said, 'Sure.'"

Jenkins: I noticed her watching the show, of course. The eye went right to her because not only were the cameras on her a lot, but she's beautiful. She's not only that, but very bubbly, as she is now. Nothing has changed. She was smiley, happy, and just open.

Plus she's Chicago, so I knew she didn't play around basically. So when I would travel I would always call or send a note or bring something back from my traveling.

Years later Nieci still has jewelry, T-shirts, and other items Tomi sent her while traveling with Cameo. The two never married and they had other relationships over that time, but they have remained close. "I've always loved Tomi," she said, "but sometimes you have to let people go, and you come back together when you're more mature and you're more settled, because I'm a no-nonsense person, and he's a good boy now."

On episode #221 of the 1977–78 season, Smokey Robinson was the headline attraction. The secondary act was a baby band from Dayton, Ohio, named Lakeside, who had a ballad out called "If I Didn't Have You" and were on the verge of signing with Dick Griffey's SOLAR Records. But at the time they were just a bunch of young musicians from Dayton, Ohio, trying to make an impression.

Lakeside lead singer Mark Wood had two important missions that day: to perform well and to make contact with Sharon Hill, one of the most prominent *Soul Train* dancers. She'd partnered earlier with the innovative Tyrone Proctor when they'd won a contest at *American Bandstand* in 1975. During her years on the show, Hill toured the country with other dancers as the Soul Train Gang and was regularly featured in *Right On!* magazine.

Wood's band was the product of a fantastic, underappreciated music scene in Dayton that would produce the Ohio Players, Slave, Roger and Zapp, and many other dynamic funk bands. So when they hit LA, Wood knew the band had chops. It was just a matter of paying dues. Getting on *Soul Train*, of course, was a career goal, but Wood was after more. "I had seen my wife in the show," Wood recalled. "You see someone, and you say, 'That's the girl for me.' I knew one day I'd meet her. I didn't meet her until years later and we were on the show together. But I did choose her off the television." Though Wood was determined to meet her, the young performer was apparently also shy. Instead of going over to her, Wood asked Chuck Johnson to pass along his number and ask her to call. Hill wasn't interested.

"I was too busy," she said. "Chuck said, 'Please call him. Just call him.' I said, 'I was raised in Texas, and the way I was raised, with ten sisters, my morals are different than California. So I finally called him. He said everything I wanted to hear. So I said, 'Okay, we can go out.' When we did it, we were like two peas in a pod. It was like we were meant."

Five years after that first date, they were married and have had four children, two boys and two girls. Lakeside would enjoy its biggest sales success with the 1980 album *Fantastic Voyage*, the title track of which would be an R&B hit and then, redone by rapper Coolio in 1994, a top-three pop hit. The band still tours, and the singer and the dancer have lived happily ever after.

Chapter 15
AHMIR THOMPSON:
SOUL TRAIN FANATIC

|||||||||||||||||||||||||||

IT IS a twenty-first-century Thursday night in hipster heaven: Williamsburg, Brooklyn. At a converted factory turned bowling alley/restaurant/nightclub named Brooklyn Bowl, a thousand revelers fill the dance floor. The crowd is mostly white but with a healthy percentage of blacks, Asians, and Latinos, dancing, drinking, and engaged in various forms of seduction.

Looking down from an elevated DJ booth is Ahmir Thompson, known as Questlove, the drummer and leader of the hip-hop band the Roots, as well as musical director for Jimmy Fallon's popular late-night NBC comedy show, a gig that has made him one of the most visible figures in popular music. He's emerged as an in-demand DJ who gigs all over the world (schedule permitting), but he rarely misses this Thursday-night party, which he titled Bowl Train.

This homage to *Soul Train*, along with Thompson's trademark Afro, are not the only things that link him to the groovy 1970s.

Unlike so many contemporary music makers who are, at best, ignorant of the past and sometimes too arrogant to look back, Thompson was profoundly shaped by his viewing of Don Cornelius's brainchild. "The biggest love in my life, more than any career or woman—my mom probably places on top of that—but *Soul Train* is probably the biggest love of my life," Thompson said passionately. "This show was my MTV, my BET. Things that people younger than me now take for granted, having access to music shows when they want it."

Thompson grew up in a house of music. His father, Lee Andrews, was the lead singer of Lee Andrews & the Hearts, a classic Philadelphia doo-wop group that had several hits, their biggest being "Tear Drops" in 1957, which reached No. 20 on the pop chart. Along with his wife, Jacqui, Andrews would also be part of a soul-era group called Congress Alley. Not fond of babysitters, the couple brought their son along with them to nighttime gigs and on tour. By age seven Thompson was drumming as part of their show, and by thirteen he was arranger and musical director for his parents.

Despite this background, his parents enforced a very firm 8:30 bedtime for him, a rule that conflicted with the late-night airtimes of all the music shows, especially *Soul Train*, which came on at 1:00 A.M. on Philadelphia's CNBC, a UHF channel. Because they were a musical family and their son loved music, they'd allow Thompson to get up at 12:50 A.M. to watch the show downstairs in the dark.

The show-opening animation "actually scared the living daylights out of me," he remembers. "It was hands down some of the most evil, engaging animation. I was so frightened and excited about the show all at the same time, and so it just became an obsession. There was no rewind button. The Betamax didn't come out until 1979, so you pretty much had to use your memory to memorize everything." Thompson wasn't allowed to watch cartoons or sitcoms until he was thirteen, so *Soul Train*, and other music shows, were his childhood

TV world. "Obviously, it affected me, because, you know, I go absolutely nowhere in this world without three computers and a bunch of hard drives with every *Soul Train* episode that I've ever collected in the last twelve years—because I show people," said Thompson. "I force them [to watch] at gunpoint."

Eventually, *Soul Train*'s popularity in Philadelphia got the broadcast shifted to noon. As a result, Thompson was joined in his *Soul Train* viewing by various family members. "I guess I was the alarm," he recalled. "There's always that one person who had to let everyone know the segment before the *Soul Train* line came on. That was my job. *Soul Train* came on at twelve o'clock, so I guess the line was at twelve forty-five after the support act does their second song. You pretty much have to yell, 'Aunt Sherrie! The *Soul Train* line is about to come on!' They would gather around and watch it like it was old-time radio. I was the designated alarm, like the ice cream man was coming."

As he became a teenager, Thompson's *Soul Train* obsession grew stronger. He had to see every show—even in the face of punishment.

Thompson: Sometimes I had to weigh out the consequences if I got caught—am I willing to take an extra two weeks on top of what I got already? And you know, the answer is always yes. Usually on punishment weeks, I would have to just ease my *Soul Train* jones. We're talking the early eighties. I would have to really devise a MacGyveresque-like system to watch the show. By Tuesday I would have to find a designated person in my school to record the show for me, so once off punishment, I could have access to what I missed—but that wasn't good enough. You figure I would just leave well enough alone and say, "Okay, in three weeks, once my grades get better or whatever, I'll watch the four episodes I missed." There was no feeling in the world like eleven fifty A.M. on a Saturday when you know that your all-time favorite show is about to come on.

You prep for it. You make sure everything is done. I make sure that my lessons were done, my drum lessons. I would take seven A.M. class on Saturday and get all that out the way and be home at eleven fifty just to be home and catch *Soul Train*. On weeks that I was on punishment, I would have to tell my next-door neighbor, who was also an avid watcher, to raise his volume up just a little bit so I could hear it through the wall. So I would press my ear against the wall and, if that wasn't enough, next week I'll tell him, Leave your bathroom window open, because I can see directly into their guest room. Turn on the guest television. They had a big television, and for some reason it worked.

So Thompson could either watch it and not hear it or hear it and not watch it. "It's one thing for your best friend to agree to it, but it's another thing for your best friend's parents to wonder why they're blasting a *Soul Train* episode on two televisions at the loudest levels ever," he said. "You know they'd always turn it off. I'd yell, 'Turn it back on!' He'd say, 'My mom made me turn it off.'"

Whenever that happened, Thompson turned his friend into his designated recorder.

Thompson: I'd basically ask for a play-by-play of what happened as if it were a basketball game. Which, you know, by this point my obsession got to the point where it was past the dancing. What could you really ask about *Soul Train* details? What did Rosie Perez look like? Or what song did New Edition perform? The things that I was obsessed with most of *Soul Train* are the details. There were two episodes I was on punishment for that, coincidentally, Don *had* to choose the episode that I was on punishment for. He tried two new ideas. One was he did sort of a clear animation of the show. So instead of the normal intro where it's clearly an animated sun and black background that eventually morphs into the studio, they did, I guess, two episodes in which they use some sort of digital effect so you can see both the studio and the animation going on at the same time. This is torture, because I'm not allowed to watch this for three weeks.

That was the kind of stuff I was obsessed with. I wanted him to tell me how the digital box came down when announcing that Al Green was performing. How long did it stay there? Morris Day and Al Green have the longest record of seconds, the digital box. The digital box is what they show you when the guest is on. "*Soul Train*, the hippest trip in America. Guest stars Evelyn "Champagne" King, Grandmaster Flash and the Furious Five, and the *Soul Train* dancers!" One episode, and I don't know why, but Morris Day stood there for like eight seconds. "With guest star Morris Day." I was like, "Are you sure it's eight seconds?" I made him get on the telephone. He said, "Listen to it." That's how crazy my obsession got.

Because Thompson held on to his Afro well past the hairstyle's 1980s expiration date, everyone in his neighborhood associated him with the Jackson Five.

Thompson: I do remember the day that Michael Jackson premiered the robot on *Soul Train*. Only because it was similar to the effect he had ten years later when he did the moonwalk on *Motown 25*. All my cousins, all next door, they saw it, and just instantly you had to do the robot. They would ask you, "What do you want to be when you grow up?" Because I held on to my Afro the longest of any adolescent, they'd be, "Yeah, you wanna be the Jackson Five." I thought being the Jackson Five is more of an occupation than a birthright. No, I'm not gonna go through the loins of Joe and Katherine. I'm just gonna apply for the job.

Thompson's reaction to seeing James Brown on a 1974 show had humorous consequences. "That was the first time I saw James Brown control a microphone," he says. "You know, watching him toss it back and forth. The only object that resembled a microphone, at least something with a pole and a platform to it, was our toilet plunger. So I would practice with a toilet plunger. Then my dad would be, 'Boy, do you know where that has been?' I would just drag it around the house, pretending that that toilet plunger was a microphone. Finally my dad was like, 'No, you can't play with this no more. It's a hazard.'"

While legions of fans around the world are obsessed with *Soul Train*, few have been able to so directly translate what they learned from the show into their work. For Thompson, "the shows that the artists were able to display their skill live were probably the most important performances on *Soul Train*. As far as live performance is concerned, hands down I believe that Al Green takes the cake. Actually, he has three live episodes. Many people don't mention his 1972 performance where he did 'Love and Happiness' and did Kris Kristofferson's 'For the Good Times.' Very powerful performance."

Questlove was working with neo-soul star D'Angelo on his masterful 2000 *Voodoo* album and the dynamic tour that supported it. "At the time I had that episode, I was working on D'Angelo's *Voodoo* album. When D and I were talking about how to craft the live show, we always noticed that Al Green sort of made a very big moment out of silence and the fact that he would touch the band and sing with the mic at arm's length away and sort of project clearly. The fact was that silence was just as loud as him screaming—those are tricks. We pretty much used a bunch of *Soul Train* episodes to sort of craft his *Voodoo* tour."

On one *Soul Train* show, the New York funk ensemble Mandrill marched "in from the audience with the cowbells," he recalled. "I mean, that's a trick that the Roots and I still use to this day. We use that Mandrill episode as a template. Also Junior Walker and the All-Stars in '71. He does a very good cover of Chicago's 'These Eyes.' Just a real funky cover of it. They're so good that I actually digitized it so that I could DJ with it, because it's that funky."

You'd think with his intense love for *Soul Train*, it would have been a dream come true for Thompson to appear on *Soul Train* with the Roots. But his feelings about that moment were complicated. "My love for *Soul Train* is much more than just, 'Oh, I wanna play," Thompson said. "Eventually I got my chance to play, and it was anti-climactic, as I thought it would be. We made it to *Soul Train* in 2000, and Don was all types of confused about it. We brought both Jaguar Wright, unknown, and Jill Scott, unknown, to the show to perform two separate songs. So there was confusion there, because it was like one artist was gonna get an interview and one artist wasn't gonna get an interview. They decided that Jill's performance was more engaging, so they decided to conduct the interview behind that. But then they thought she was a member of the Roots. They didn't know that was the future Jill Scott onstage."

In preparing for that performance, Thompson "took a cue from the Beastie Boys."

Thompson: The Beastie Boys were the only act I knew clever enough to actually go in the studio and make a track for them specifically to lip-synch on *Soul Train* so that it would appear to be live. So we wanted to do—at least I wanted to do—the same thing.

My band isn't as on fire with *Soul Train* as I am. I didn't want
my only appearance on the show to be lip-synching. Especially
when we're called the best live act in hip-hop. So I spent four
days crafting the sessions that would be for *Soul Train*. I wanted
to meticulously remember everything. I said, "Don't over-ad-lib,
because then you're gonna come off like Marvin Gaye, forgetting
your cues and all that." Marvin was world famous for just letting
the track go and not singing to it. We got there and I was trying
not to get excited. But naturally, of course, you get there and you
get excited. And it was just over in a huff.

After years of viewing the show, the drummer's interaction with
the legendary host, while pretty typical of Don, proved disappointing.

Thompson: My only interaction with Don Cornelius was,
"Son, you can't stand there." "I'm sorry." Like, I wanted to be
the fly on the wall that just stood in the back of the show and
watched. I think I was watching Sisqo doing "The Thong Song."
I saw Don and I told myself, I'm gonna do the very thing that
irks me whenever fans come up to me and wanna talk. They're
very passive sometimes. They'll be so scared to speak that they
stand behind me, not say anything, and act like they wanna say
something but not say it. I was like, You're not gonna be that guy,
you're not gonna go behind Don Cornelius and start geeking
out and tell him stories. He actually walked up to me and was
like, "You can't stand here," and walked away [laughs]. Everyone
felt bad for me more than me. I shrugged it off. I get it. I wasn't
allowed to stand there.

Considering that Questlove has watched as many *Soul Train* episodes as anyone, who delivered his favorite performance? Was it Al Green? Patti LaBelle? Or maybe Marvin Gaye? As a man who walks the line between soul and hip-hop, trying to bring them together in his work as a producer and DJ, it's not so surprising his choice is New Edition, a Boston-bred quintet that also walked that line.

Thompson: I mean, there's probably nothing better in the world of soul music than to watch choreographed moves done to the tee and absolutely clean and 100 percent precise. I'll say that New Edition, in performing on that show, had an advantage above the Jackson Five, even though the Jackson Five is the standard and the mold that New Edition followed: I'm under the impression that New Edition not only had to master the Jackson Five appeal and their mold but, in creating their own mold, had to sort of base it on hip-hop choreography, which is probably the most complex choreography of black music. The fact that you have to utilize your head, using different levels of B-boying and break-dancing. You just never, ever saw a group cleaner than New Edition. Of course, in the subsequent reunion tours of New Edition, you'll always see that Bobby Brown was always his own drummer. He would sort of, in a defiant move, not do the choreography that they're all supposed to do, but there was one point in time, Bobby Brown absolutely was in sync with Ronnie DeVoe, Ricky Bell, Ralph Tresvant, and Michael Bivins, and it just, really—it got no better.

DANCER PROFILE: Nick Cannon

The hosts of the Soul Train Awards over its twenty-year run tended to be mainstream figures—Luther Vandross, Gladys Knight, Patti LaBelle, and star-turned-movie-star Will Smith. But only one Soul Train Awards host both danced and performed on the show. It's not to say that Nick Cannon's other credentials aren't impressive (star of the film *Drum Line*, host of shows on MTV and Nickelodeon, married to Mariah Carey), but he has a unique position in the *Soul Train* history. His relationship to *Soul Train* echoes that of dancers from the 1970s and 1980s while also illustrating the changes time made on the brand.

Growing up in San Diego, Cannon remembered that "*Soul Train* is embedded in the black household, so you come out the womb watching *Soul Train*. That's when you knew the cartoons were over, because *Soul Train* was coming on. So you done . . . you been sitting in the spot for four hours and you know you get to exercise your bones when *Soul Train* comes on. When *Soul Train* went off, it was time to go outside and show everyone the moves that you just learned from *Soul Train*. You created your own *Soul Train* after the show went off with your friends in the neighborhood. You out there popping and locking and trying to battle and do what you just saw. So if it was Jody Watley, getting it popping. If it was New Edition, hearing the songs for the first time—it was like a visual radio station for us."

Like many viewers who watched the show in the late eighties and early nineties, Cannon's favorite person on *Soul Train* "was hands down Louie 'Ski' Carr, because he was just so cool the whole time, just whole eighties. My man had the glasses on. He would walk around with the cane and he was in everybody's video in the eighties. He hung out with everybody. He was just mad cool. He had this swagger the whole time."

Cannon may have grown up in the eighties—a decade after the show first started airing—but he still saw *Soul Train* "as the tastemaker for all black people at the time. That's where you saw the newest acts. I mean, you might have heard the song a couple times on the radio, but *Soul Train* was the first time you got to see them live in living color. You'd see how they perform, see how they interact, see how they handled Don's tough questions, and that made you a fan. I was happy to say that [almost] all of my music I purchased as a youngin' was because of *Soul Train*."

What's also fascinating is despite his youth, Cannon was steeped in *Soul Train* lore. Growing up in the era of the VCR, he was able to see tapes of some of the classic 1970s episodes that are essential to the *Soul Train* legacy—and he saw them as part of *his* legacy. "Everyone from Marvin Gaye to Al Green knows those classic performances that we've seen on *Soul Train*," Cannon said. "For someone like me who really is a performer, all my recollection goes back to seeing those performances. So really it has inspired generations of performers, people who may not have had the opportunity to see those performances originally, but that are all in the archives of *Soul Train*. We gotta know about when Marvin Gaye performed on *Soul Train* or when Al Green sang live with the audience around him or when Stevie would come on. That's the blueprint on how to do it today."

By age fifteen Cannon, ambitious and multitalented, was already hanging around LA "trying to be an entertainer. I was doing everything, from stand-up to rapping and dancing. And being a fan of *Soul Train* and watching it every day, being like, 'Wow, that's Hollywood, people are always up there. Once I get to LA, I gotta go audition to be on *Soul Train*.'"

The process of getting on *Soul Train* in 1995 for Cannon wasn't very different from the process on getting on *Soul Train* in 1975 or 1985.

Cannon: You gotta stand in line all Saturday morning. You gotta be the best dressed you could possibly be, fresh all the way on. Literally, someone comes out and starts pointing at people to start to come in, and you like sittin' there like it's the gate to heaven to get to be chosen to be on. Eric was the guy who came out. He was an older brother who'd come out and, obviously, he'd pick all the fly chicks first. We'd be like, "Tell him to pick me once you get in there." Then, you know, if you had that right persuasive lady or however it was, you could get Eric's attention—that's how you got in. I would see him and start dancing and start practicing and making sure my outfit was all the way fly.

This was early nineties, so I was wearing shiny shirts with the matching Hush Puppies. I had on a shiny lime-green shirt and matching shiny lime-green Hush Puppies, trying to get chosen. One day he pointed at me. Once you get the recognition, once you get christened by Eric, you could come back as long as your outfit was fly. So once I got in, it was on. You couldn't get rid of me. I was showing up every week that they was taping. First it's getting through the door—once you get through the door and you're in the building, you become part of that sea of dancers that you only get to see the top of their head when you watch *Soul Train*. You don't necessarily get to see what they got on or what they doin', but they are in the crowd.

Then once you get through there, you might make it to the edge of the stage. Then, 'cause you ain't center stage just yet, but you get to dance in the rafters, and the camera might hit you, and then . . . you get to actually dance on the stage if you get to that level. Then once you get from dancing on the stage, you get to be part of the *Soul Train* line. That's, like, that's the star moment is when you actually get to go down the *Soul Train* line. I remember it would be weeks, it would be months, and I'd be like the next dude getting ready to go down, and I'd be ready to kill it, and they'd be like, "Cut!" And I'd be like, "Dang. I didn't make the *Soul Train* line this time." I actually only made it one time. I only made it down the *Soul Train* line one time, and that was just the highlight of my fifteen-year-old life.

Cannon danced on the show during the post–Don Cornelius period, so he doesn't have any of those funny and fraught tales of interacting with Don while trying to get a better spot on the dance floor. Tommy Davidson, then a hot comic, hosted a show Cannon attended. Actress Rhona Bennett, who was on the notoriously bad sitcom *Homeboys from Outer Space* and later *The Jamie Foxx Show*, made a more lasting impression. They got to talk when Cannon did the scramble board, and "as the years went on we became friends, and I knew her for a long time and stuff. She had a record deal, and we would do music together." Bennett would be part of the vocal group En Vogue from 2003 to 2008.

Cannon: The scramble board, for a young teenager, is probably like the SATs, just because of the type of pressure that it's set up for. I mean, number one, it's national television, so I know my mama gonna be watching, my auntie gonna be watching, so I better spell this word right, 'cause you know my family's legacy is on the line. "That boy gonna get on there, and he can't spell and gonna let the world know he's dyslexic," so you got that whole pressure. Then you gotta make sure you look fly, 'cause then, you know, they ask you your name and stuff. So at the time I was a rapper, so I had to give him a fly name. I told him I was Nick Knack, or something crazy like that. I didn't really use my real name. They pair you up with some lady that you don't know, so I had to hope that her intelligence level was on high, too, so y'all don't mix the word up. I remember my question was one of the greatest golf prodigies of all time, something like that. As you all know, it's Tiger Woods. I was sitting there like, All right, how many g's are in *Tiger*?

Though he wasn't in the studio the day Mariah Carey made her debut on the show, he vividly remembers his future wife's appearance on *Soul Train*. "You know what, being a youngster and seeing her perform 'Vision of Love' on *Soul Train*, I was like, 'One day, I'm-a be her vision of love. Watch. I promise," he recalled. "She was definitely one of the people that when she graced the *Soul Train* stage, everybody was talking about it, you know, right after. 'Yo, you see that girl?' That was like the first time for me and many other people that actually saw her perform live, and she was so natural and comfortable and fine. You know it was one of those things—light-skin girl with the curly hair. Ooh, I want her. And I spoke it into existence."

The personable and ambitious young man started a rap duo called Da G4 Dope Bomb Squad in his teens that was getting opening-act slots with bigger groups around Southern California. After that broke up, he was signed to Jive Records, where the label hoped that he'd be the next Fresh Prince. He believes the *Soul Train* experience was crucial in getting him into the music game.

Cannon: For one, I thought I was on national television, so that was on top of my résumé. I'm like, "I'm a *Soul Train* dancer, you can catch me at Paramount Studios every week." You get a chance, you know, if you're a cool cat, you get a chance to meet every artist that kinda comes through. Most of the artists just hang out. I mean, I was always intrigued by the way a production works. So I was, you know, getting close with all the cameramen and the producers, just trying to figure out what goes into the process of creating a show. And you're right there, you're right at the pulse of the music industry, so everybody is coming through there. I created a lot of friendships when I was a young cat. People I still see and talk to today.

I was always a young kid with ADD, and, to me, the production was fascinating. I mean, when you see *Soul Train* on television, it's like this huge 360 world, and then you get there and it's a regular soundstage. And you're like, "Wow, so this is how it looks," and then I started wanting to know more about camera angles, and why do they shoot up? What's the crane do? How does that lens make it look so massive and stuff? So I would just ask questions and the entire crew was always nice enough—I think they saw this kid that was wide-eyed and just ready to obtain as much knowledge as possible. They would just talk to me about it. You know, I thank all those people that kinda took the time out to explain stuff like that to me. Now being the one that's the producer who creates a lot of content, it's one of the things where I just naturally think of what I was taught on the set of *Soul Train*.

In 2003, his debut self-titled album was released with a single produced and written by R&B's reigning king, Jive Records label mate R. Kelly, called "Gigolo" that was a minor hit. So, like Patrice Rushen, Jody Watley, and Jeffrey Daniel, Cannon joined a small group of folks who danced on *Soul Train* as a teen and returned as a performer.

Cannon: It was like coming full circle. I mean, because being a kid I was standing outside in the cold trying to get in there just to see the set, just to dance, just to do whatever. And then to actually— you always hear about what the dressing rooms look like up there, and to actually be in one of the dressing rooms chilling and walk the artist walk, all of that stuff, it was amazing. I literally was like, Wow. That was one of those moments in my career where I thought, "Okay, I'm actually doing it. I'm actually living the dream that I always dreamed of." So it was special for me. I couldn't contain myself. It was one of those things where I was just excited and hyped. I don't know how that affected my performance at the time, but I was definitely overhyped.

"Gigolo" is no classic, but with R. Kelly producing and Nick at that point appearing on the Nickelodeon show, "it was one of those smashes that just kinda came out of nowhere . . . I was just joking around when we created the record, because I was obviously on kids' television at the time." The idea of Cannon as a gigolo was obviously tongue in cheek.

Cannon: But the beat was crazy. I remember R. Kelly putting the beat on, and I was like, "Yo, I'm-a take that in the other room and record something to it." I wasn't thinking I was recording a single or even something for my album. I was just like, "I'm-a do my grown-man thing on this. I'm-a talk about chicks. I'm-a talk about my life, all of that." There was no hook on it or anything. It was just me rapping. And, like, you know, sixteen bars with three verses. And I left the studio, came back a couple weeks later—actually I hadn't come back, I got a phone call from the record label, like, "Yo, that record 'Gigolo' that you and R. Kelly made is insane." I was like, "I ain't record no record called 'Gigolo.'"

Kelly got inspired by the lyrics and wrote this "Gigolo" hook. And it just became a hit. So by the time we got to *Soul Train*, that was the first time that I actually understood that it was a hit record. Before then I thought it was just a record that we did that was fun. They talked about picking it as a single. Then I got to the stage and saw people singing along with it. That was my first time actually performing that record. It was crazy. I knew I was good.

Performing on the show, Cannon finally came in personal contact with Don Cornelius, the goal of every *Soul Train* dancer. Though by then Cornelius had retired as host of the weekly show, he was still very much a presence in the studio.

Cannon: When I was a dancer on *Soul Train*, you gotta have your A-game on. So by the time I was an artist and this dude that we always saw walking the halls, hands in his pocket, who you might not want to make eye contact and get kicked off the set—then you actually got the opportunity to talk to him, and you're like, Damn, this is such a nice, loving dude.

It was one of those things where it was like an opportunity where I really was like, Wow, to get that, to actually have that moment where, man, Don Cornelius knows my name. To be able to share that experience and then to create a relationship with him. I mean, like, he's definitely someone I call on when I need a favor or some advice. It's one of those things where I would never dream of that one day, him calling, asking me to host one of the award shows. I felt like my career just jumped leaps and bounds, to go from revering this man to actually having a personal relationship with him.

Cannon hosted the Soul Train Awards in 2005 along with singer-songwriter Brian McKnight, *American Idol* star Fantasia, and tabloid star Nicole (daughter of Lionel) Richie. But instead of holding it in Pasadena or Santa Monica, the show was held, perhaps in a cost-cutting move, on the *Soul Train* soundstage. But the Cali native did more than just host. In 2005 he'd formed his own label, Can I Ball Records, and released a single called "Can I Live?"

Cannon: The record was dealing with the fact that my mom was a teenage mom, and that she'd been advised to have an abortion, and the record kind of came from a perspective of me speaking to my mom from her womb, saying, you know, "Can I Live?" It actually made a huge impact, you know, in politics, and it was a great record. I won a lot of awards for it, but to me, my memory from that record was actually getting to perform that record onstage at the Soul Train Awards. We had like forty kids wearing "Can I Live?" T-shirts. I remember looking at the audience and seeing my mom like bawling, and tears, and I said, "Aw, ain't gonna cry. Gonna keep my performance together." But that would be one of the moments that I will always remember; I thank *Soul Train* so much for giving me that opportunity, because that was the only show that I was able to perform that record live on.

If *Soul Train* returns to television in any form, Cannon expects to be its future host.

Cannon: I always see *Soul Train* as that destination for our culture. Whatever was going on in African American culture you saw on *Soul Train* for many years, you know what I mean? That's something archived. When aliens come in about two thousand years and they want to see what was going down in black life, they could watch all episodes of *Soul Train*, and they'll see that's how we got down. Our fashion, the way we walk, the way we talk, the way we move, what type of music we listen to, what was going on in politics—all of that was in an episode of *Soul Train* from before I was born all the way to the present day. That was a destination that you could kind of turn to to see us. You could see who we are—you know, it wasn't the watered-down version that you might see on a sitcom. Or it wasn't, you know, it wasn't the negative depiction of us that you might see on the news. It was us having a good time and enjoying each other.

Chapter 16
SOUL TRAIN AWARDS

||||||||||||||||||||||||||||||||

FOR MANY decades, civil rights leaders and entertainers sought a nationally televised prime-time show that would celebrate black achievement in general, and black music in particular. The Black Music Association, the organization I had first traveled to LA to cover in 1981, had made the production of such a show one of its stated goals. But none of the big three networks—CBS, ABC, NBC—would touch it, despite the huge crossover success of Michael Jackson, Prince, Lionel Richie, and Whitney Houston in music and Eddie Murphy, Richard Pryor, and Bill Cosby on television. Black stars occasionally had their own TV specials or summer replacement shows on networks while also being featured on the Grammy Awards and telethons like Lou Rawls's annual benefit for the United Negro College Fund. But nothing existed just to celebrate the rich spectrum of black music.

Don Cornelius had tried in various ways to extend the *Soul Train* brand through his short-lived Soul Train Records and by managing O'Bryan. Perhaps, with this history in mind, he first pitched a fifteenth-anniversary *Soul Train* show and not something annual. He approached his partners at Burrell Advertising, and they were open to it because of how valuable Cornelius had become to their clients.

Michelle Garner, who'd watched *Soul Train* growing up in Chicago, joined Burrell Advertising in 1985 and was immediately impressed with Cornelius. "He was a great marketing partner for the business," she said. "He really served as a visionary to us because he was in the music business, and at the time I worked on the Coca-Cola account, and Coke had a music marketing strategy. So we were using lots of talent for our classic commercials and would talk all the time . . . Don was very involved in things we were doing with Coke. "He would make suggestions talent-wise, or this song was getting ready to hit, or this artist was getting ready to blow up. Just things we needed to be on the lookout for. I love him dearly, even though he did kick me off *Soul Train* when I tried to get on there and dance one time. He wouldn't let me dance, so I was little bit disappointed. But I've gotten over it."

Though they weren't able to pull off a fifteenth- or even a sixteenth-anniversary special, when Cornelius came to Burrell about starting an annual show, Garner supported it immediately. "I just knew it was gonna be huge, and I signed on the spot. I said, 'Yes, we're in.' I didn't even talk to the client . . . From an agency standpoint, at Burrell we got all our clients aligned with that property, and that helped launch it. With Coke we actually negotiated soft-drink exclusivity and, I think, we maintained that until it went off the air."

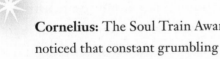

Cornelius: The Soul Train Awards came about because we had noticed that constant grumbling from people of color who didn't feel that they got the respect they deserved from the established awards shows. So we saw an opportunity through the Tribune Entertainment Company to create a show that focused on black talent and the best performances for a given year. It would be a party that focuses on us, part of a party that we barely got invited to. That was the whole point of it. It gave us a tremendous amount of joy from 1987 through the next twenty or so years. The first Soul Train Awards in 1987 offer a somewhat amusing window into the state of black music that year. The great Stevie Wonder was given the first Heritage Award, and Janet Jackson won best video for her dancing in the iconic "What Have You Done for Me Lately." Run-D.M.C. won two rap awards. Cameo, an old-school funk band reconstituted as a new-wave-influenced, video-savvy trio, won for the single and album titled *Word Up!*

The humor was provided by the two awards captured by one-hit wonder Gregory Abbott, a pretty-boy vocally challenged singer who, aided by technology, won (hilariously) both best new artist and best male singer. Over the years the Soul Train Awards would exist as an erratic barometer of quality, with truly worthy winning plaudits next to minor, transitory talents. Though the program began in 1987, after the peak of Michaelmania, Michael Jackson has won far and away the most awards, with twenty. Sister Janet has thirteen, but as the show continues on, expect current hit makers Beyoncé, Usher, and Alicia Keys to challenge the Jacksons.

USUALLY HELD in an auditorium in Pasadena, the Soul Train Awards became noted for the enthusiastic, sometimes rowdy crowds that sat in the balcony. While the seats in the orchestra were primarily reserved for entertainers, business insiders, random celebrities, and others connected to the entertainment industry, the balcony became a West Coast equivalent of the Apollo Theater. When performers hit the stage, especially those with youth appeal or up-tempo songs, they had to play to the rafters if they wanted any real energy.

Aretha Franklin's legendary career was the inspiration for the Soul Train Lady of Soul Awards, a TV special first held in 1995.

Sometimes the judgment handed down by the balcony gods could be cruel. At a 1989 Soul Train Awards appearance, Whitney Houston was actually booed by many in the balcony, an apparent commentary on her song choices. Many fans of R&B resented her reliance on big pop ballads, feeling she was turning her back on black listeners to cater to white audiences. Still, it was quite stunning to hear Houston so publically chastised. Don himself took the stage to defend the singer and reprimand the crowd. Though Don had been critical of the crossover mentality of the era, he was too gracious a host (and understandably concerned about booking stars in the future) to let the disrespect pass.

The Soul Train Music Awards show was successful enough that in 1995 Cornelius launched another annual special, the Soul Train Lady of Soul Awards, which focused on female vocalists and achievers and enjoyed a ten-year run. These award shows would be Don's most successful spin-offs from the weekly show and, in fact, would have serious cultural currency even as the weekly show was running out of steam.

It is noteworthy that in 1993 it was Don Cornelius's idea that Burrell reach out to BET about hosting a promotional event tied in with the broadcast. "After the first Soul Train Awards, we decided to make Sprite the lead brand in that property and did a consumer promotion," Michelle Garner said. "So we actually initiated the promotion in 1988, and the winners went to the 1989 Soul Train Music Awards, and we sent close to a hundred people from all over the country, and we had a big party the night before with all the winners. After a few years, we had invited celebrities, and they would come, but then it started to wane off, and Don suggested that we bring in BET to televise the party."

As a result, a pre–Soul Train Awards event called Sprite Night was created. It was a live two-hour music concert that went on for six years and was quite successful for all involved. However, this collaboration between the two most important brands in promoting the visuals of black music wouldn't be enduring.

In 2001 the network launched its own show, the BET Awards, with a broadcast out of Las Vegas. But afterward the BET show, like the Soul Train Awards, would be shot in LA and would celebrate the best in black music while adding categories covering TV, film, and sports to the mix, allowing the program to cast a wide net in terms of booking talent and attract a wider audience. With BET nationally available in every major market and firmly established as the chief vehicle aimed at black viewers, the BET Awards quickly dwarfed the Soul Train Awards as the most significant celebration of black culture.

While on a daily basis the BET Awards catered to young viewers, BET embraced adults as well. Unlike the Soul Train Awards, which had to rely on syndication and were thus subject to the whims of local television stations, BET controlled what time its award show aired and how often it was repeated, giving it a major competitive advantage.

Chapter 17

NEW JACK SWING

|||||||||||||||||||||||||||||||||||||

ON EPISODE #436 of the 1983–84 season, New Edition would make its first *Soul Train* appearance to perform "Candy Girl," the hit single off their debut album on the independent Streetwise Records. The five Boston adolescents (Bobby Brown, Ralph Tresvant, Michael Bivins, Ronnie DeVoe, Ricky Bell) were adequate, singers—at best—but they had a scintillating stage show that married aspects of old-school Temptations-style choreography with hip-hop-generation dance steps. It was a unique blend that mirrored the pseudo-soul tracks produced by their mentor, Maurice Starr, which contained rap breaks and some beat-boxing. Only the most visionary *Soul Train* viewers could have imagined that they were watching not only a highly entertaining performance but a band that embodied the immediate future of black music. Over the course of the next ten years, R&B music would be sonically and thematically absorbed by hip-hop. First it would just be rap breaks on otherwise typical R&B tracks. But soon a generation of producers, born into older black music traditions but who came of age in the 1980s, would fuse the beats and samples of hip-hop onto sing-along melodies.

The men of New Edition—among them Bobby Brown, who was at the start of a hit- and headline-making career—would be messengers of the new movement. "*Soul Train* was probably the one show that I, for some reason, foresaw myself being on," Brown said. "Being a dancer with New Edition, I told them, I was like, 'One day, we're gonna be on *Soul Train*,' and all of them talked about me, they called me all kinds of names."

The five came together through Boston talent shows where, under the guidance of choreographer Brooke Payne, they developed a dynamic stage show. "We were part of the dance-crew scene," Brown said. "When hip-hop first got started and break-dancing and pop locking, we were there. I was the best dancer in all of Boston. When it came to battles, I won probably all of them. I only lost one battle ever in my life, and it wasn't against somebody from Boston, it was against somebody from New York. So I still hold the title in Boston."

Famously, New Edition invited Big Lou onstage with them, much to Don's displeasure. Brown even made mistakes on that first performance because he was spending more time watching Big Lou than focusing on Payne's routine. "Yes, I messed up a few times," he acknowledged. "I was probably the one in New Edition that at least had four mess-ups per show. I think that's probably why I went solo. Because I wanted to do my own thing anyway. I would sometimes do my own move on purpose, throw my own move in there, and the guys would laugh. That's what it was about, us having fun onstage."

New Edition's members were so young that Cornelius asked the five what they planned to do with their money.

Brown: All of us guys were talking about, "I'm gonna save my
money. I'm gonna put mine away for college." I was just like I
wanted to do with everything. I actually said, "I'm gonna spend
mine." Being on the *Soul Train* set, the vibe is cool. All the
dancers are getting themselves together. It's a real laid-back type
of set, and then once the music starts, all hell breaks loose and
everybody is just trying to do the best dance so that they can get
camera time.

Brown, though barely out of puberty, made the women of *Soul
Train* a focus of his dancing with the pelvic thrust that would become
a trademark. He recalled gleefully, "Oh, the girls! They always reacted
nicely. We liked that. You gotta throw a pump in there every once in
a while doing a step. You throw in a pump to get the girls excited."

Following that debut, New Edition would become the subject of
a bidding war when they were able to escape their contract with small
Streetwise Records. The quintet ended up on West Coast–based
MCA Records, which was then becoming a major player in black
music. While their original producer, Maurice Starr, went on to control the lucrative careers of New Kids on the Block, a white Boston
teen group that utilized the same musical formula as New Edition,
New Edition went on to have major hits with "Cool It Now" and
"Mr. Telephone Man."

Despite the new record deal and becoming the first vocal group
with hip-hop appeal, there was great turmoil within the group.
Three of the members remained a tight unit (Bivins, DeVoe, Bell)
while Tresvant and—to a much greater degree—Brown were outli-
ers. Brown didn't just mess up steps on purpose; he was often late for
appearances, group meetings, and shows. It all came to a head at the
end of 1985 when Brown was voted out of New Edition. Signed as a
solo act by MCA, Brown would release *King of Stage*, his debut album,

in 1986. In retrospect it was a transitional album, as he worked to find his own voice as a singer. During this period he'd work on choreography with Rosie Perez and continue to refine his R&B/hip-hop hybrid.

By 1988, an inevitable fusion of R&B melody and hip-hop beats was labeled "new jack swing" by *Village Voice* writer Barry Michael Cooper. Acts like Keith Sweat and Al B. Sure! would beat Brown to the marketplace in 1988, but his *Don't Be Cruel* album would sell some nine million copies and establish him as the hottest male entertainer of that era.

Brown: New jack swing is basically soulful hip-hop. It's singing hip-hop. It is rap music with vocals. You put rap and singing together, and that's what new jack swing is. Than it's a real hard beat. It's a banger for you. It's something to dance to, and it's got slick bass lines. I think we just basically took what Zapp, Gap Band, Parliament, Funkadelic did and we put it into a rap format and made it work.

Backed by new jack swing–pioneering producer-writer Teddy Riley and the West Coast–based team of Kenny "Babyface" Edmonds and Antonio "L.A." Reid, *Don't Be Cruel* was one of the definitive albums of the time, and its success made it clear that new jack swing was the new direction for dance music. *Soul Train* was a happy home for new jack–influenced artists. The 1987–88 season featured Riley-produced MCs like Heavy D & the Boyz, Keith Sweat, Al B. Sure!, and Guy (which Riley was a member of). The last show of that taping season put the final stamp of new jack's arrival with New Edition, Bobby Brown, and future Brown replacement Johnny Kemp on the same show. Throughout the next few seasons Boys, LeVert, Troop, Today, Tony! Toni! Toné!, Johnny Kemp, Lisa Lisa and Cult Jam,

Full Force, After 7, Jeff Redd, and many other acts with new jack swing records made regular appearances.

Some of the most innovative uses of the new style came from three of Brown's old band mates. Bell Biv DeVoe released their debut album, *Poison*, in 1990, combining elements of new jack swing with a distinctive, idiosyncratic sound that spawned two massive hits, "Poison" and "Do Me Baby." They had a rougher, more streetwise look than New Edition, one that would influence up-and-coming acts like Jodeci and R. Kelly and lead directly to the absence of the suit-and-tie look among that era's vocalists. Bell Biv DeVoe appeared on *Soul Train* episode #628 during the 1989–90 season with a Bobby Brown video and, incongruously, soulful jazz singer Randy Crawford.

Bivins would, as he matured, become one of the more successful talent scouts of the 1990s, finding M.C. Brains, ABC (Another Bad Creation), and, most important, Boyz II Men, a Philadelphia quartet that would become the biggest pop vocal group of the decade. Brown's recording career would sputter following *Don't Be Cruel*, but he'd become tabloid fodder following his 1992 marriage to superstar singer Whitney Houston. In keeping with the *Soul Train* theme, the Brown-Houston romance got its start when they met at the 1989 Soul Train Awards.

New jack swing would be the last great innovation in R&B music before hip-hop became the mainstream of black pop music. Moreover, it would be the last big movement in the music he loved that Don would preside over as *Soul Train*'s host.

Chapter 18

NEW HOSTS

AT THE dawn of the 1990s, the Los Angeles that gave rise to *Soul Train* was receding into history, and love, peace, and soul was not on the city's agenda. Tom Bradley, the black mayor elected in the aftermath of the Watts riots and serving the last of five terms in office, was generally viewed as a distant figure by both white and black residents, totally out of touch with Los Angeles's current challenges. Complaints of police brutality against members of the black community, not dissimilar to those voiced back in the sixties, intensified as the LAPD waged war against the Bloods and Crips, two loosely organized gangs whose reckless gun violence had claimed thousands of lives since the introduction of crack cocaine to the metropolis in the mid-eighties. Some days the *Los Angeles Times*'s Metro section read like dispatches from a war zone. LA-based rappers like NWA, Ice-T, and Ice Cube had made the region seem like a powder keg in their recordings.

These rhymes proved prophetic when, in the aftermath of Rodney King's beating by a crew of policemen and their subsequent trial and acquittal, an uprising and riot starting in late April 1992 sent shock waves through the city and the nation. Many of the city's enduring black institutions found it hard to survive in this contentious new environment. One significant casualty was Maverick's Flat, once one of Los Angeles's hottest entertainment destinations but now, like many of the businesses on once-bustling Crenshaw Boulevard, finding business crippled by the fear of gangs and guns. The club, so essential to the birth of *Soul Train*, would float in and out of operation throughout the nineties.

Quietly but steadily, black folks were beginning to abandon LA, either moving east to the more affordable Inland Empire or back down South, where their families had originally migrated from, an exodus that continues to this day. Just as a slew of movies suggested (*Colors, Boyz N the Hood, South Central, Menace II Society*), the City of Angels was no longer viewed as a promised land for working-class black families, but rather as a ghetto with sunshine.

In the world of black entertainment on TV, there was great change afoot, the roots of which go back to a *Soul Train* taping in 1981 when Arsenio Hall, a young comedian from Cleveland, made his first national TV appearances, performing stand-up on two episodes. Throughout the 1980s, Hall, a tall, big-eyed man with a conspiratorial delivery and an easy laugh, built his career in comedy and developed close bonds with other young comedians including Robert Townsend, Keenen Ivory Wayans, and superstar Eddie Murphy, forming a loose collective who'd be labeled the Black Pack by the news media. Hall came to national prominence in 1986 when he hosted the last two seasons of the long-running syndicated dance show *Solid Gold*. In the late 1980s, when Fox began its efforts to launch a fourth television network, a career-changing opportunity would come Hall's way. The network started *The Late Show* to compete with Johnny Carson's long-running *Tonight Show* on NBC. When Fox clashed with original host Joan Rivers and she quit, it tried several replacements in her slot before giving Hall a shot. Over the course of thirteen weeks, Hall developed a balance of contemporary irreverence, black slang, and old-school TV host obsequiousness to bring a fresh take on late-night television.

Fox, which had invested heavily in black talent with the shows *In Living Color* and *Roc*, should have locked Hall into a long-term contract; instead Hall slipped away, and in 1988 he played a key supporting role in the Eddie Murphy comedy *Coming to America* before signing on with Paramount for his own syndicated late-night show. Debuting in January 1989, *The Arsenio Hall Show* was, for its time, as important as *Soul Train* had been nearly twenty years earlier. During the broadcast's five-year run, Hall captured the glamour of black popular culture at just the moment that hip-hop was going pop, new jack swing was invigorating R&B, and a wave of black film was creating new stars.

Though he didn't feature dancers, Hall's show made great use of his Los Angeles home base and his intimacy with the stars of the age, from Murphy to Prince to basketball's Magic Johnson to starlets like Paula Abdul. He embraced hip-hop's talents, giving Snoop Dogg, MC Hammer, and many others their first serious national exposure. When Magic Johnson wanted to talk to the nation about acquiring the HIV virus in 1992, he chose to sit down with Hall. When Bill Clinton was running for president, he went on Hall's show to play sax and burnish his image.

While not direct competition for *Soul Train*, Hall's cutting-edge style as the host of a popular black show made Cornelius's enterprise seem locked into an outmoded black hipness. So at the start of the 1993–94 season, after hosting *Soul Train* for almost twenty-five years, Don made the fateful announcement that he was exiting his on-camera role. When asked what finally pushed him off the stage, Don cited the example of Jim Brown, the great running back who quit the Cleveland Browns after winning the National Football League championship in 1966.

"Jim Brown, the Hall of Fame football player, is a good friend," Cornelius said. "I always admired him for having the courage to get out of the game before somebody said retire. People didn't have to say, 'Why don't Jim Brown hang up his cleats?' I was afraid of someone saying, 'Why don't that old brother Don Cornelius put the microphone down and let somebody else do that?' I ran into people that said, 'Man, you should still be hosting the show, because you're good.' I think to myself, that's the one who would be saying, 'Why don't that old brother put down the mic and get off the stage.' That's the one."

In theory, it was a smart move. Cornelius had little emotional connection to any of the acts then appearing on the show, and quite a few were young enough to be his grandchildren. But replacing himself was easier said than done. Though *Soul Train* would continue on air for another thirteen years until 2006, you could argue that when Cornelius left the podium, the show was over.

Episode #735 of the 1993–94 season was the first not hosted by its founder and producer. Kim Wayans, a star on Fox's *In Living Color* and the female member of the comedic Wayans clan, would be the first to attempt to fill his spot. The rest of that season's thirty-one shows would be hosted by comedians (Steve White, Lewis Dix, John Witherspoon, George Wallace), actresses (Sheryl Lee Ralph, Paula Jai Parker, Ella Joyce), actors (Mario Van Peebles, John Henton, Morris Chestnut), and one very poised model with a TV future (Tyra Banks).

The 1994–95 season would be heavy on models, with Banks returning and a long list of beauties to follow: Karen Alexander, Roshumba Williams, Lana Ogilvie, Veronica Webb, Beverly Peele, Gail O'Neill, Cynthia Bailey (a future *Real Housewife of Atlanta*), Michelle Griffin (who would go on to marry the Roots' Tariq "Black Thought" Trotter), and Waris Dirie. If you were black, tall, and had appeared in *Elle* magazine or the J.Crew catalog, you could have hosted *Soul Train* that season.

But just because Don was offstage, it didn't mean he wasn't still an on-set presence. Gail O'Neill, a very proper Jamaican American girl from New York who had a long career in modeling and later as a TV host, doesn't remember many details of the show she hosted (episode #783). Nor does she remember the three acts featured (69 Boyz, Tanya Blount, Y?N-Vee). What she does remember is Cornelius hovering around and not interacting much with her until she voiced a few complaints.

"I saw these cute little girls with low-slung pants," O'Neill recalled, "and I could see their G-strings. I pointed that out to someone, and Don was immediately, 'They need to pull up their pants.'" The model also objected to the scramble board question about a man "who married and murdered. The answer was O.J. Simpson, and that was very distasteful to me. Don had the question changed." Despite being on a show that was still on TV around the nation, O'Neill recalls getting more reaction from appearing in the J.Crew clothing catalog than from hosting the show, a reflection both of how few blacks were still appearing in mainstream fashion and how much the show's impact on pop culture had fallen. She was paid around $2,000 for hosting, a check that wasn't sent to her agent but arrived at her apartment in a handwritten envelope. "I thought it was junk mail 'cause it didn't have a return address and was handwritten," she said. "But my doorman opened it and said there was a check inside." O'Neill, who has gone on to appear on network shows and hosted a program on the H&G network, is glad she did *Soul Train*, but it isn't a memory she reflects on very much.

Though the show lacked Cornelius's on-camera presence for most of the 1990s, it was still a strong attraction for emerging artists. Among those anxious to appear on *Soul Train* were a female vocal trio from Houston named Destiny's Child who had a single out in 1997, "No, No, No," that featured Wyclef Jean. Mathew Knowles, father of lead singer Beyoncé and the group's manager, was pushing to get his new group on *Soul Train*, but "Don's policy was that you had to have an album out before you can be on his show," and the album wasn't scheduled for release until February 1998.

> **Knowles:** So what we cleverly did was package "No, No, No" with Wyclef as the second song. The moment I met Don, and he talked to me, he was feeling me out. In his deep voice: "I like you. You are going to do really good in this industry." I guess he saw something in me and we connected from that moment. He smiled at the fact that we were clever in getting Destiny's Child on *Soul Train*. That was Destiny's Child's first-ever TV performance.

Mathew Knowles was a huge *Soul Train* fan, and it was appointment viewing in his Houston home. Not surprisingly, *Soul Train* pops up in the careers of two performing daughters. Beyoncé, wearing a 1970s Afro, did a *Soul Train* parody scene when she appeared in 2002's *Austin Powers in Goldmember*, while Solange's second album, *Sol-Angel & the Hadley St. Dreams*, has a retro 1970s soul sound, and the supporting videos were vibrant *Soul Train* tributes. That connection between the Knowles family and Cornelius would eventually benefit both as Destiny's Child and, later, Beyoncé would be honored with multiple Soul Train Awards as well as lifetime achievement awards.

Among the many emerging stars who'd make their first national television appearance on *Soul Train* in the nineties were up-and-coming stars Erykah Badu and John Legend. But with every year the number of stations carrying the show seemed to shrink, and its longtime distributor, Tribune Entertainment, became less committed. Following the 1996–97 season, Don abandoned the host-by-committee approach and went with a series of hosts who'd handle the duties for a season or two. These Don replacements would include comic Mystro Clark, soap opera heartthrob Shemar Moore, and actor Dorian Gregory, none of whom had the gravity, charisma, or flair to make the show cool again—or to shake Don's shadow. Meanwhile on BET, first Donnie Simpson and later a series of youthful female and male hosts on the daily broadcast of *106 & Park* became the new Don Cornelius as they broadcast hit videos on the national cable channel and became the de facto faces of televised black music.

The 1,117th and final original episode was televised on March 25, 2006. But through 2008, episodes of classic shows from 1974 to 1987 were still in syndication, testimony to the truth that *Soul Train*'s past was richer than its present.

Chapter 19

SELLING SOUL

IIIIIIIIIIIIIIIIIIIIIIIIIIIIIIIIII

KENARD GIBBS has vivid memories of growing up in Chicago and watching the local version of *Soul Train*. "My mother was a school-teacher and she knew many of the kids on the show from her high school English class," Gibbs fondly recalled. "She'd say, 'That's Betty. No wonder she was all dressed up today.'" For years Gibbs has treasured these moments he shared with his mother, never suspecting that one day he'd own a piece of *Soul Train*. He'd tell this story to Don Cornelius some forty years later as they were negotiating the sale of the television show. At Williams College, Gibbs befriended another future black media entrepreneur in Peter Griffin. They stayed in touch as Gibbs attended Northwestern to get his master's in business, worked for advertising giant Leo Burnett Worldwide, and then served from 1999 to 2006 as the president of Vibe/Spin Ventures, LLC, where he oversaw both the magazine and several television ventures (an award show, a weekly lifestyle show).

So when Gibbs left to start his own business, he hooked up with Griffin and Anthony Maddox, a former business advisor to Sean

Combs, to form MadVision Entertainment. The trio got a TV deal at Showtime for a half-hour show titled *Whiteboyz in the Hood* and a DVD deal with Lionsgate studios, and they were working on a deal to aggregate black content online when they went in search of additional funding to expand. At the recommendation of Vibe CEO Robert Miller, the MadVision partners met with executives at InterMedia Partners, a private equity group founded in 2005 with seven funds aimed at investing media properties in cable, publishing, television, and broadband.

That initial meeting was cordial, but MadVision's need for $7 million was just too small a deal for InterMedia. If MadVision had a serious acquisition, they were told to come back. Just before the meeting broke up, Gibbs mentioned how valuable the *Soul Train* library was. "There are very few libraries like it," Gibbs explained. "It was a unique asset. At the time Don had only allowed fifty-two episodes in syndication. That meant some eleven hundred or so hours of shows had been shown only once. That's thirty-five years of history."

The downside of the *Soul Train* library is that Cornelius had not made rights deals other than for the shows' initial airing. To exploit these episodes, buyers would have to clear all the music masters and song publishing. Still, the all-white executives of InterMedia, all old enough to have seen *Soul Train* in its prime or at least aware of its reputation, were excited by the opportunity. So MadVision reached out to Cornelius's longtime business advisor Clarence Avant.

The timing of their inquiry was perfect. Sometime in 2006, during the period when *Soul Train* was doing its last broadcast, Cornelius had decided he'd sell the brand outright if the right offer came along. Avant cites an incident involving Mary J. Blige as the tipping point. She was supposed to meet with Cornelius, "but she never called, never showed up," said Avant. "After thirty-five years of the longest-running syndicated show on TV, Don began to realize, despite all of the people he had helped, the music scene had moved on. He told me, 'I want you to get me out of this shit.'"

Three Japanese businessmen and their interpreter came to Los Angeles to meet with Cornelius and his son Tony, but the gathering was a bust. "After listening to thirty minutes of the pitch in Japanese, Don said, 'Tell them there is no deal, no kinda way," Avant said. Time Warner, when Richard Parsons was its chairman, had shown serious interest. "Parsons called up and introduced me to the cable distribution guys. We met four times. Don was very excited by it. Don wanted a *Soul Train* channel." However, those talks ended when Parsons stepped down from his position at Time Warner at the end of 2007. There was a feeler from black-owned TV One, but Cornelius wasn't interested. Similarly, MTV Networks expressed interest, but, again, Cornelius didn't want to meet with them. Of his friend, Avant said, "If Don didn't wanna do something, it wasn't gonna happen."

So when MadVision appeared on the scene, *Soul Train* was still available. The roadblock was the plain-spoken Avant. "I didn't want Don to sell to them," he told me. "I wasn't convinced these young guys would be able to put together a strong enough deal." Even after the MadVision team and InterMedia senior partner Peter Kern flew out to meet with Avant, the veteran dealmaker wasn't sure. Finally he took them seriously, and they went back and forth on the deal for nine months.

"Don was very reserved during the back-and-forth of the negotiations," Gibbs remembers. "The best part for us was to have lunch with him and just listen to him tell stories about the show. I don't think he really believed it would happen until the money hit his account." Cornelius called the three MadVision principals in May 2008 when the deal was done. "He told us we must carry on the *Soul Train* name, and that he appreciated the fact that we could get this done," said Gibbs. "Don was already a rich man, but this was a life-changing transaction."

In the years since InterMedia financed the MadVision purchase of the *Soul Train* brand, a lot has changed internally. While maintaining equity in Soul Train Holdings, Griffin and Maddox are no longer actively involved in managing the asset. InterMedia sold a substantial share of its *Soul Train* equity to one of Magic Johnson's funds, enough so that the basketball great turned businessman is now chairman of Soul Train Holdings.

In terms of sustaining the brand's relevance, the deal is still a work in progress. The Soul Train Awards have been revived on BET's adult-oriented Centric Channel. VH1's documentary *The Hippest Trip in America* (from which many interviews in this book were culled) not only was a ratings winner for the network but has played in film festivals around the globe. An annual *Soul Train* cruise has proven popular and, in the District of Columbia, *Soul Train*–themed lottery tickets went on sale in 2013.

But the big dream of Soul Train Holdings is to bring the weekly show back. Reality TV wizard Mark Burnett was involved at one point, but he couldn't sell his concept. "Our goal is to have *Soul Train* on a network," Gibbs said. The old syndication model that *Soul Train* used is outmoded in the twenty-first century. "We wanna keep some of the elements that made the show a classic, but make it a contemporary show that can compete with *American Idol* or anything else on the air today."

A big issue for any *Soul Train* reboot is dealing with how social dance is now spread via the Internet. The explosive and, thankfully, brief life of the "Harlem Shake" videos in early 2013 aptly displayed how a novelty dance can travel the globe. Ditto "Gangnam Style," a dance video by Korean MC Psy that blew past one billion views on YouTube and spawned more tribute videos than there are people in Montana. For innovation in black dance, the place to be is definitely YouTube, where new regional styles are uploaded and then imitated nationally. A great example is jookin', a balletic Memphis-bred style of movement that incorporates *en pointe* (in sneakers) alongside elements of old-school popping and locking with hints of hip-hop breaking. Dancers like Lil Buck have gone from battles on Beale Street to performing with classical cello superstar Yo-Yo Ma via his remarkable videos.

Director Kevin Swain interviews Don Cornelius for the 2010 VH1 documentary *The Hippest Trip in America*.

Since late in 2012, Magic Johnson has become more of a spokesman for the *Soul Train* brand, going on TV and radio to talk about his hopes for its future, speaking both about trying to launch a new weekly show and pursuing a biographical film about Don Cornelius. The basketball great, who two years ago brokered a deal to buy baseball's Los Angeles Dodgers, is an able businessman with impeccable contacts in the entertainment and business worlds. He is well positioned to fulfill the mission that MadVision began in acquiring *Soul Train*, but time will tell.

Chapter 20
THE HIPPEST TRIP IN AMERICA

||||||||||||||||||||||||||||||||||||

WHEN DON Cornelius sold *Soul Train* in the spring of 2008, he was seventy-one years old. He was a rich man who'd just become a very rich man. What would he do with all this new leisure time? He talked to several writers (including myself) about helping him write an autobiography, but apparently it was never completed. There were conversations about a *Soul Train* movie, but that didn't get traction at any studio. He met with John Singleton and pitched a *Soul Train*–themed television show, using the *Soul Train* tapings as a setting for tales of Los Angeles during the seventies. It was a promising concept, but it, too, got lost in the Hollywood wilderness, a place where black-themed series in the twenty-first century were now as rare as they were pre–Diahann Carroll's *Julia*. In many ways the book Don never wrote was the VH1 documentary *The Hippest Trip in America*, which was the highest-rated entry in the network's Rock Doc series. In 2009, Cornelius was the first person interviewed by the episode's director, J. Kevin Swain. It was a three-hour interview, and while nothing was expressly off-limits, Don didn't want questions about his personal life, and, as we've seen, he didn't want to get into his long-ago issues with Dick Clark.

Don Cornelius, 1936–2012. Rest in peace.

The dynamic dances first showcased on *Soul Train* live on around the globe.

It was a very relaxed interview, largely because of Cornelius and Swain's relationship. Swain had worked in production on fifteen Soul Train Awards shows, from the late 1980s up to 2003; he had also been involved with two Soul Train Lady of Soul broadcasts and one comedy special that Cornelius produced for syndication. "We had a kind of father-and-son relationship," Swain said. "I was always getting into trouble and being called into the office by Don, being sat down and told, 'I'm gonna tell you what you did wrong this time.'" For years Cornelius had always told Swain, "as long as you are on my set, I'm the boss," but on the day of the shooting, he was on Swain's set, where Swain was the boss. "Don told me, 'I guess you are the boss now,' and was very good about it."

It was quite a challenge to squeeze all those years of television shows into sixty-four minutes. Chaka Khan got one line. Sly Stone got one line. Patti LaBelle, two lines. Two key friends of the show, Gladys Knight and Stevie Wonder, could never get scheduled during the six-month shoot and edit. The producers could never pin down Oprah Winfrey. Cornelius very much wanted Marvin Gaye represented in the documentary, because Don considered him one of his closest friends in the business. But according to Swain, Cornelius was "appreciative of [the final film]. Believe me, Don was not one to bite his tongue. If he didn't like it, we'd have known."

Having known his subject as a boss for over a decade, it's interesting to hear Swain's take on Cornelius post–*Soul Train*. He said, "At the interview and whenever I saw him, he was upbeat and smiling. Looked like a burden had been lifted." Along with Cornelius, Swain did a number of promotional events for the documentary, including a 2011 Don Cornelius weekend in Chicago where a Don Cornelius Boulevard was named. "Don just seemed to be having a good time and was very open whenever he spoke in public."

"I'd see Don around Los Angeles in the years after the documentary. I'd see him at Neiman Marcus with his wife, shopping and eating. He'd drive around with a young wife and his yellow Rolls-Royce, and they looked like a very happy couple."

The Hippest Trip in America has been aired on VH1's Viacom sister stations, BET and Centric, as well as shown at festivals in Berlin, Barcelona, and two cities in Brazil, Rio de Janeiro and São Paulo (though because of the many music-clearance issues with the show, it has yet to appear on DVD or Blu-ray). Despite those limitations, Swain is convinced "the doc cemented the legacy of the show. What a great, great show it was. Now you know what we really miss."

Chapter 21
LAST DAYS

||||||||||||||||||||||||||||||||||

IF YOU Google images of Don Cornelius and Viktoria Chapman, you'll see a gallery of red-carpet photos of Don in well-tailored suits and designer glasses, his salt-and-pepper hair cut into a dignified curl (far different from his huge Afro days). Viktoria is a pale, statuesque Russian blonde in a tight-fitting dress with lots of visible cleavage. They were married in 2001 and make a handsome May-September, ebony-ivory couple. In Beverly Hills circles, couples made up of older rich men and younger beautiful women are as common as palm leaves falling onto convertible car hoods.

There isn't much known about Chapman's background. She is a former Miss Ukraine who modeled in Russia and had a daughter, also named Viktoria, from a previous relationship. She apparently appeared in a couple of soft-core porn films before meeting Don. Even folks who knew Cornelius well apparently didn't get to know her well. "It was Hollywood," said one old friend. "No one cares, really."

That may be true in general, but certainly in the case of *Soul Train*'s founder, there were many who questioned the marriage. But for several years the relationship seemed to be working, and the two were often seen at his longtime haunts, like the Beverly Hills Hotel, where he had a charge card and a regular table.

Unfortunately, Don did not spend his retirement years in quiet contentment. Around 2004 Rosie Perez, by then an established actress, was dining at Spago in West Hollywood when he walked over. He was there with his wife, and he was very happy to see Rosie. They exchanged phone numbers, and she called him the next day. "We laughed about our run-ins and stuff that happened on the show," Perez said. But her overriding memory of the conversation was "that he told me he felt very lonely."

In 2007, Chapman filed for divorce and had two restraining orders placed against her husband. In 2008 he was arrested at his Mulholland Drive house after being pepper-sprayed by Chapman multiple times following a heated argument with his estranged wife. In court records, he's quoted saying, "Although she instigated the confrontation by shouting insults and profanities very close to my face, and even though the incident itself involved mutual acts of aggression against me, her injuries were very apparent. My injuries were to my eyes and face and not apparent because of the darkness of my skin."

He was formally charged with spousal abuse and initially pleaded not guilty before changing his plea to no contest. Cornelius was placed on thirty-six-month probation, was ordered to take a fifty-two-week domestic battery course, do three hundred hours of community service, and stay one hundred yards away from the site of the incident. Their divorce became final in May 2009. "I am seventy-two years old," he wrote in court papers, "I have significant health issues. I want to finalize this divorce before I die." In the settlement, he was ordered to pay $10,000 a month in spousal support, buy his ex-wife a home not exceeding $1,095,000, and pay tuition fees for his adopted daughter.

In the wake of the divorce, Cornelius's health, physical and mental, was a focus of his friends. He was definitely suffering. He moved more slowly. Spoke more slowly. Couldn't drive anymore. Yet outwardly his spirit seemed strong. Businessman and longtime friend Danny Bakewell had lunch with him in December 2011 and recalled, "We were talking about family and friends. It wasn't about how terrible everything is. I didn't get the impression he had any major health problems or concerns." Longtime supporter and soul legend Gladys Knight told CNN, "Last time I saw him, he was pretty sick. He had lost a lot of weight, but he still had that thing about him." Clarence Avant, who dined with him the day before Don died, recalled Don being in the same good mood.

But Don, an icon of cool who'd learned long ago to mask his inner life when necessary, was clearly not at peace. Some speculate that the very messy divorce shattered his self-confidence and embarrassed him. Others suggest his failing health, including a cancer scare and lingering effects of his brain surgery, made him despondent. Or perhaps he was just uncomfortable with getting old.

Late on the night of February 1, 2012, Tony Cornelius received a phone call from his father. "It was a call of urgency," he told CBS's Gayle King, "and I came to his home immediately." When Tony arrived, he found his father lying lifeless on the floor. Police were called around 4:00 A.M. and found Don with a self-inflicted gunshot wound to the head. His body was taken to Cedars-Sinai hospital where, at 5:00 A.M. on February 2, he was pronounced dead. Don Cornelius was seventy-five.

Don's body was cremated on February 9 and the funeral service was held two days later inside the Forest Lawn Memorial Park's Hall of Liberty, where a three-hour service featured tributes from the celebrity world Don thrived in, including words by Smokey Robinson, Jody Watley, George Duke, Cedric the Entertainer, and Barry White's widow, Glodean. The Reverend Jesse Jackson, his old friend from Chicago, delivered an affectionate and lengthy eulogy, but he captured Don's importance quite succinctly with these two lines: "He's right up there with any civil rights leader. He gave people a chance to feel good about themselves."

The Grammy Awards were to be held the next day in Los Angeles, and the show's producers were preparing a short tribute to Don Cornelius for the telecast. But the tragic death of Whitney Houston at the Beverly Hills Hotel the night of February 11 forced the producers to put together a hurried tribute to the multiplatinum pop superstar that preempted the memorial for Don. He was an innovator in the business, but Houston was a huge star who died a tabloid death. Given the difficult choice, the people behind the show went with the bigger name.

The next day, across the continent, outside in the dead of winter, a party was held at the base of a set of steps associated with a fictional fighter that proved a heartfelt memorial. In front of the Philadelphia Museum of Art, at the bottom of "the Rocky steps," over the course of four hours, a couple thousand people danced to the sounds of DJ Touch Tone in a *Guinness Book of World Records* record-setting *Soul Train* line. MFSB's *Soul Train* theme started things off, but jams like Chuck Brown's "Bustin' Loose," the Jacksons' "Can You Feel It," James Brown's "Funky Good Time," and Maze featuring Frankie Beverly's "Before I Let Go" kept the party flowing.

The mayor of Philadelphia, Michael Nutter, a baldheaded, goateed, fifty-four-year-old black man who grew up with *Soul Train*, started the proceedings with a collective chant of "We love you Don Cornelius!" followed by his version of the show's trademark "We are on the *Soul Train*!" opening. The mayor didn't dance, but he did go down the makeshift dance floor—really just two strings of rope lined up half a block long—and glad-handed in prime campaign form.

The *Soul Train* line record of 211 had been held by students at a Berkeley, California, high school. That might not seem like a lot of people until you consider that the *Soul Train* lines on the show itself probably never had that many people lined up, and perhaps only a quarter of that number actually made it on air.

The dancing this time was not spectacular. There were no Tyrone the Bones or Don Campbells or Jody Watleys or Rosie Perezes in the bunch. Most were, to some degree, bundled up. But there were some bold folks who wore Afro wigs in place of wool caps and bits of glitter along with gloves. They were mostly black, but whites, Asians, and Latinos were among the folks who shook, shimmed, and slid down the line as they were phoned, videoed, and counted for the persnickety folks at the *Guinness Book of World Records*, who would officially certify 291 of the thousand or so who danced.

Not as well publicized but just as powerful was a tribute to Don organized by Marco De Santiago and held at a reopened Maverick's Flat, where several generations of *Soul Train* dancers shared stories and danced hard and long to classic tracks. Damita Jo Freeman, Tyrone Proctor, Thelma Davis, Don Campbell, and most of the dancers who made the show famous showed up at their old haunt. A highlight of the evening was Lakeside's Mark Wood performing "Fantastic Voyage" with his wife, Sharon Hall, and the other dancers joining him onstage as if the classic funk jam captured the spirit of the wonderful experience they'd all shared. The dancers vowed to meet annually at Maverick's Flat to celebrate Don, *Soul Train*, and their continuing sense of community. Many of these same dancers have been contacted by the Smithsonian Institution about contributing clothes and memorabilia to the new African American history wing to open in a few years, a prospect that fills them with pride.

All this activity, organized by fans and folks who lived *Soul Train* firsthand, reflect a warm looking back and a fun sense of nostalgia, but not a signal that the show's legacy will endure. Yet that would be a shortsighted view. Daft Punk, two visionary French electronic dance music producer-writers, released *Random Access Memories*, 2013's hottest album, which was a rich blend of classic seventies and eighties grooves with twenty-first-century electronic flavor. The past and present mesh beautifully in Daft Punk's work. Inspired by the album, some clever video archivists reached back to *Soul Train*'s rich catalog of movement and meticulously matched them to the rhythms of Daft Punk's "Get Lucky" and "Give Life Back to Music," putting the genius of Damita Jo, Jeffrey Daniel, and the scores of unknown but equally funky *Soul Train* dancers at the service of cutting-edge music. Hundreds of thousands have watched these videos at this writing, the majority of them young people from around the globe. The dance, the clothes, and the spirit of *Soul Train* still captivate, and they will, through live events and clever online video use, live on whenever people feel the need to boogie.

ACKNOWLEDGMENTS

|||||||||||||||||||||||||||||||||

Thanks to *Soul Train* documentary director Kevin Swain for his gracious assistance. Richard Gay and Brad Abramson of VH1 were great partners. Naomi Bragin, street dance scholar, gave me wonderful guidance. Ashley Mui helped with tons of details. Special thanks to my editor, Henry Ferris, and my agent, Sarah Lazin, for making this project happen.